Rick O'Brien's interest in curiosities has two origins; as a child he saw the Roman remains at St Albans and has been fascinated by ruins ever since; and, on coming to teach in Norfolk, he has been intrigued by the numerous decayed castles, abbeys and churches contained in the county, many of which he has since researched further, catalogued and drawn. The research required for *East Anglian Curiosities* has enabled him to cast his net even wider, and during the year spent working on the book he has visited literally hundreds of potential curiosities in the three counties in order to make his selections.

Frontispiece
The Elveden Memorial (see No 28)

East Anglian Curiosities

Rick O'Brien

THE DOVECOTE PRESS

First published in 1992 by The Dovecote Press Ltd
Stanbridge, Wimborne, Dorset BH21 4JD

ISBN 0 946159 97 1

© Rick O'Brien 1992

Phototypeset in Times by The Typesetting Bureau Ltd
Wimborne, Dorset
Printed and bound in Singapore

Reprinted 1994

Contents

1 First English Authoress
2 Duel to the Death
3 A Decayed Famous Priory
4 Mill in a Gatehouse
5 Pingo Ponds
6 Norfolk Giant
7 Little Domesday Book
8 Two Towered Abbey
9 Kett's Oak
10 Nosey Parker
11 Withburga's Spring
12 A Clown and a Collapsed Bridge
13 Hitler's Sapling
14 A Medieval Tower
15 Side Saddle Introduced
16 The Oldest Man-Made Norfolk Curiosity
17 Nelson's Other Column
18 Pyramid Mausoleum
19 Curious Clock Tower
20 The Moved Church
21 Buried Treasure
22 Tower of Cubes
23 The Shattered Maid's Heart
24 Haunted by a Fiddler
25 Detached Church Tower
26 Killed by a Pinprick
27 Saxon Shore Roman Fort
28 Where Three Parishes Meet
29 A Gypsy Grave
30 Book Bound With Murderer's Skin

31 The Smallest Pub

32 Memorials to Unfortunates

33 Floating Turtle Clock

34 Old Plague Stone

35 A Bishop's Fantasy

36 Victim of the Poll Tax

37 Medieval Bell-Cage

38 The Tattingstone Wonder

39 Saint-Maker of Holbrook

40 A Tudor Eccentricity

41 A Tower for Study

42 'Old Grog'

43 An Elizabethan Conduit

44 England's Last Working Tide Mill

45 A Gothic Folly

46 Heroes of the Skies

47 Fortress Against Napoleon

48 House in the Clouds

49 The Vanished City

50 Four Headless Horses

51 St Edmund's Cursed Bridge

52 Where the Conqueror's Barons Lived

53 A King's Hiding Place

54 To See Forty Churches

55 Dick Turpin's Birthplace

56 Soldier of Fortune

57 Robert Adam's Towers

58 Unjustly Executed

59 Locks and Stocks

60 A Victorian 'Cholera Pump'

61 A Warning to Sailors

62 Bacon for the Bride

63 House of Curios

64 Evidence of a Siege

65 A Tower called 'Jumbo'

66 The Pub in the Wall

67 Merry Old Soul

68 Obelisk to Bloodshed

69   Minories Folly

70   The Kaiser's Gift

71   Felsted's Hooved Woman

72   Most Evil Essex Man

73   Tallest Gatehouse

74   Leviathans Over Essex

75   Chapel on a Roman Wall

76   Oldest Wooden Church

77   King Harold's Resting Place

78   A Victorian Spiderman

79   Memorial to a Horse

80   A Fantasy Grotto

East Anglian
Curiosities

N

CROMER

20

18

3

2

13
4
6

KING'S LYNN
23
24

NORFOLK

11

25

21

26

NORWICH

1, 10, 14, 15   GT. YARMOUTH

12

27 17

19

8 9

22

5

16

52

LOWESTOFT

THETFORD

DISS

50

28

51

49

NEWMARKET   29

30-34   BURY ST EDMUNDS
35

SUFFOLK

46

48

47

43

44   45

54

36

IPSWICH

53

42

SUDBURY

55

38 41
39

56

37

40

70

57

58

FELIXSTOWE

59

60

COLCHESTER

63-69

62 71
72

61

73

ESSEX

74

CLACTON

CHELMSFORD

75

77

76

59

78

79

BRENTWOOD

59

80

74

7

SOUTHEND

0   20

MILES

Introduction

East Anglia's three counties, Norfolk, Suffolk and Essex, are rich in historical and geographical wonders. A varied landscape has been shaped by the profound influence of invaders from across the sea who settled in this region. Romans, Anglo-Saxons, Danes and Normans have each left their mark, as did later generations of East Anglians. Items in this book reflect some of these legacies spanning the Stone Age to the Second World War.

In taking the strange and fascinating as our subject, we are faced with an abundance of curiosities. I have attempted to include a variety scattered throughout the region. There are Ice Age ponds, a vanished city, a giant's tomb, follies, unusual buildings, ghosts and legends. Some are visually arresting while others are products of tales, mystery or personal adventure.

I am grateful to the following for help with this book: Clive Wilkins-Jones, who suggested that I take on this project; staff of Norwich Central Library, Local Studies Department; Margaret Smith, Christine and David Stabler, and helpers at Parham Memorial Air Museum.

For permission to publish photographs, I thank Bungay Castle Trust Ltd; Colchester Museum; Corporation of London (Wanstead House Grotto & Grosvenor Memorial) as Conservators of Epping Forest; Eastern Counties Newspapers Ltd (illustrations from the *Norfolk Chronicle and Norwich Gazette*); English Heritage (Burgh Castle is an ancient monument in their care); The National Trust (Burlington Mausoleum, Duelling Stone & Ickworth House); St Edmundsbury Museums; Geoff Gostling, T. Hare, Sylvia Le Comber, Christine Cooper, the owners of Layer Marney Tower, and special thanks to the keepers of all the churches whose wealth of curiosities I have used. Donations to these establishments during visits would be most appreciated.

Finally, I would like to dedicate this book to my wife Trish for all her support and encouragement.

Rick O'Brien
Norwich, 1992

Mother Julian's Cell.

1 First English Authoress

Position: St Julian's Alley, Norwich.
OS Map: Norwich and the Broads, Sheet 134, 1:50,000.
Map Ref: TG 235 082.
Access: By car from Rouen Road (parking at church); by foot from either Rouen Road or King Street.

Attached to St Julian's church in Norwich is a reconstructed cell (the original was destroyed in bombing during World War II), which is the shrine to Mother Julian, the 14th century authoress of *Revelations of Divine Love*. This is the first known English book written by a woman.

Mother Julian of Norwich lived as an anchoress; one who dedicates their life to God in solitude. She was born in 1342 and lived until shortly after 1415. Not much is known of her life and we do not know her real name or background. She was articulate and clever and probably educated, though she wrote that she was 'unlettered'. She may have been associated with the nuns at nearby Carrow Abbey and could have used their library. Her thoughts and writings on God and evil are still highly regarded.

In her later life, Mother Julian was appreciated enough to benefit by bequests from wills which kept her in necessities. Her worldly goods must have been very few. The cell where she spent most of her life originally had three windows, one of which looked in upon the church and one must imagine she took comfort from being able to observe the ceremonies.

Places of Interest in the Neighbourhood
A Medieval Tower (Norwich)
Side Saddle Introduced (Norwich)
Nosey Parker (Norwich)

2 Duel to the Death

Position: Cawston, Norfolk.
OS Map: North East Norfolk, Sheet 133, 1:50,000.
Map Ref: TG 153 240.
Access: On the B1149 from Norwich, just before junction with B1145.
Marked on the map 'NT Mem Stone'.

At Cawston Heath in 1698, a duel took place between Sir Henry Hobart and Oliver Le Neve in which the former died. It is difficult now to imagine why two intelligent people should fight to the death over some name-calling; pride and honour may have been major factors. Commemorating this event is the 'Duelling Stone', erected by Hobart's son John, 1st Earl of Buckinghamshire.

Both combatants were well known locally and were involved in politics. Sir Henry Hobart, 4th Baronet of Blickling, had been knighted at the age of thirteen when Charles II visited Blickling Hall. As a powerful aristocrat in Norfolk, Hobart represented King's Lynn in the last parliament of Charles II, and supported the Revolution against James II. He was a committed and ambitious member of the Whig party.

Hobart's opponent, Oliver Le Neve of nearby Great Witchingham Hall, was a Tory and a Justice of the Peace who had inherited his wealth from a rich uncle; a very successful stationer.

In 1695 the Whigs were returned to power, with Henry Hobart in full support. Electioneering had proved expensive for Hobart and, with his father's electioneering debts to pay off, he was forced to sell some of the family estates to pay his backers.

Another election, in 1698, led to Hobart's downfall when he failed to be re-elected. He returned embittered to Blickling to dwell on the loss of his power and status. Following this, Hobart believed reports that Oliver Le Neve was spreading rumours to discredit him; one in particular, that Hobart had been a coward in Ireland during his crusade with William III, and that this was the reason he had lost his Norfolk seat in parliament. Despite any real evidence that Le Neve was responsible, Hobart became convinced of his rival's guilt and challenged Le Neve to a duel.

Le Neve wrote to Hobart denying the accusation. Hobart was headstrong and pressed the charge even further by insulting Le Neve in public. In a second letter Le Neve wrote; 'I am ready and desirous to meet you when and where you please to assign.' He was not going to tolerate insults from Hobart and would fight, despite the fact that Hobart was a better swordsman.

At Cawston Heath on 20th August, 1698, the rivals met. There they duelled. Hobart wounded Le Neve in an arm. However, Le Neve, who was left-handed, may have had an advantage. Taking a chance at the right moment, Le Neve thrust his sword deep into Hobart's stomach mortally wounding him and he died the next day.

Lady Hobart and her friends sought revenge on the victor who fled to Holland when she offered £500 reward for his apprehension. A campaign was started to have Le Neve tried and declared an outlaw. Believing he was the aggrieved party, Le Neve refused to give up hope of returning to Norfolk and proving his innocence.

Fortunately for Le Neve, a friend, Edward Lombe, was appointed Sheriff and Le Neve felt safe enough to return to Great Witchingham to stand trial. He was acquitted by Grand Jury of any blame for Henry Hobart's death and felt justice had been done at last.

Life after the trial was packed with misfortune for Le Neve. His wife, Jane Knyvet, died in 1704, and when he married Elizabeth Sheffield in 1707 she died three months later. In 1711, a tragic and saddened Le Neve died, just a few months after the death of his only son.

Places of Interest in the Neighbourhood
Pyramid Mausoleum (Blickling)
The Moved Church (Edgefield)

Stone commemorating the duel between Hobart and Le Neve.

3 A Decayed Famous Priory

Position: Bacton, Norfolk.
OS Map: North East Norfolk, Sheet 133, 1:50,000.
Map Ref: TG 350 331.
Access: Just off the B1159 coast road; marked on map as 'Priory (rems of)'.

Tucked away in the remote village of Bacton are the remains of Bromholm Priory, once one of England's richest and Europe's most famous monastic establishments. Founded by William de Glanville in 1113, Bromholm Priory never really prospered until the 13th century. In 1223, a desperate, wandering monk with his two children managed to convince the prior that he had a relic of the true cross. The monk was given a place in the priory in return for the relic. From that day onward Bromholm became rich and famous as a place of pilgrimage, especially after a visit by Henry III in the 1230s. He gave more land to the priory so that it could increase its income. In its time the relic was recorded as having raised 39 people from the dead and cured 19 of blindness. After the Dissolution of the Monasteries in 1535, the relic was lost and the priory fell into decay.

Bromholm was mentioned in Chaucer's *Canterbury Tales* when the miller's daughter prays 'Helpe Holy Crois of Bromeholme,' which emphasises its fame. Today, remnants of the church buildings can be seen in a private field, and there is an interesting gateway not far from the coast road.

Places of Interest in the Neighbourhood
Norfolk Giant (West Somerton)
Mill in a Gatehouse (Ludham)
Hitler's Sapling (How Hill)

4 Mill in a Gatehouse

Position: 3.25km/2m South of Ludham, Norfolk.
OS Map: Norwich and the Broads, Sheet 134, 1:50,000.
Map Ref: TG 381 158.
Access: From the church, take Stocks Hill south (becomes Staithe Road), at junction, take road right (to Horning & Wroxham), St Benet's is signposted at the next junction. Park near here and walk down farm road to the ruins, 1.5km/1m.

St Benet's Abbey gatehouse, with an 18th century windmill in its midst, presents a most striking composition. A curious sight indeed and not as the original builders had intended!

Attached to the gatehouse is a good portion of outer wall adjoining the River Bure. This originally bordered a small dock. Remaining foundations of the abbey walls can be traced in places around the site. In the middle of the old abbey, parts of the 14th century church can be seen on high ground. Other buildings would have included a hall, dormitory, bakery, kitchens and stables. Still visible are the long fish ponds dug by the monks and used to supply food for consumption and trade.

This Benedictine site is small now but was once a wealthy manor of about twenty-five monks, with properties in Ludham and elsewhere. Founded in 1020 by King Cnut, the stone buildings replaced earlier wooden structures erected by the Saxons around AD690. In 870, the invading Danes burnt down most of the abbey buildings.

At the time of the Conquest in 1066, St Benet's supported King Harold. Following a long attack and blockade by the Normans, one of the monks, Ethelwold, let the attackers into the abbey, thus ending the siege. Ethelwold had harboured an ambition to become abbot of St Benet's. While he was outside the secure walls of the abbey on an errand, he was taken prisoner by the Normans. Ethelwold agreed with his captors to let them into the abbey if, after its fall, they would appoint him as abbot. This they agreed upon.

The abbey surrendered when the Normans were let in. Ethelwold was promptly ordained abbot but then hanged from the gateway by the new rulers who saw him as an untrustworthy traitor. Some say Ethelwold's ghost frequently cries out and haunts the shadowy ruins.

St Benet's has the fame of being the only religious establishment not dissolved by Henry VIII. Its last abbot, William Reppes, was made Bishop of Norwich in 1536. At the Dissolution of the Monasteries he was allowed to maintain a house at St Benet's. However, by 1549 the

St Benet's Abbey with an 18th century mill in its midst.

neglected abbey fell into decay and stones from its buildings and
walls were thereafter plundered and used locally, there being no stone
naturally available in such quantities. The present Bishop of Norwich is
still abbot of St Benet's and on the first Sunday of August every year he
holds a service at the ruins.

A visit to this remarkable site is soon rewarded as 'history' can be felt
amongst the few preserved and protected remnants. It is a favourite
place for artists and sightseers.

Places of Interest in the Neighbourhood
Hitler's Sapling (How Hill)
Norfolk Giant (West Somerton)
A Decayed Famous Priory (Bacton)

5 Pingo Ponds

Position: Thompson Common, South of Watton, Norfolk.
OS Map: Thetford and Breckland, Sheet 144, 1:50,000.
Map Ref: TL 941 966
Access: Just off the A1075, between Watton and Great Hockham; park at old Stow Bedon railway station, the 'Great Eastern Pingo Trail' car park. Footpath goes to Thompson Common and along disused railway, (no dogs).

Pingos are entirely natural curiosities and near Watton there is a concentration of them unique to the British Isles. But what are Pingos?

Found dotted about this Breckland area, Pingos are small irregular shaped depressions in the land, filled with water. Formed during the great Ice Age, about 20,000 years ago, they are now homes to a variety of creatures and plants and look like soaked lunar craters. Many are hidden beneath thick vegetation and trees in this humid and damp environment.

A Pingo would have started life as a frozen mound – the ice having pushed up the soil as it solidified and expanded. In melting, the top of the hump tumbled to the edge of the mound, thus creating a crater which filled with water.

Other examples in Norfolk can be found at Marham, Walton Common and Foulden Common. Many others have been destroyed by agricultural processes.

Places of Interest in the Neighbourhood
The Oldest Man-Made Norfolk Curiosity (Grime's Graves)
Where Three Parishes Meet (Elveden)
Curious Clock Tower (Little Ellingham)

6 Norfolk Giant

Position: West Somerton, Norfolk.
OS Map: Norwich and the Broads, Sheet 134, 1:50,000.
Map Ref: TG 475 195
Access: St Mary's is down a small road off the B1159, signposted
'church'.

St Mary's churchyard, West Somerton, contains the grave of Europe's
tallest man of his day, Robert Hales. Born on 2nd May, 1820, he grew
to a staggering 7'8" tall (233cm) and weighed 452 pounds (33 stone).
His family were also very tall; father was 6'6", mother was 6 feet, his
four brothers averaged 6'3", and his sisters averaged 6'5"!

In his early career, Robert Hales went to sea but soon gave this up in
favour of touring England to show off his stature, initially with his
sister Mary who was 7'2". Tragically, she died aged twenty, soon after
going on the road.

Hales had a very eventful life following this period. At the age of
twenty, he met Queen Victoria, Prince Albert and the Duke of Wellington. Soon after that he was introduced to Louis Phillipe of France
who told the Giant he was 'Nature's chef d'oeuvre.' When he met
Queen Victoria again in 1851, she awarded him a gold watch and chain.

While touring York, Hales became involved in a dispute over some
land which he had bought. A verse was composed at the time to record
what occurred;

> At Wakefield Fair, Hales had a glorious stir,
> But he was right as soon you shall infer;
> For threats and menace will not operate,
> To sway the justice of the Giant great!
> "A plot of ground" was the disputed lot,
> Which Hales, by purchase, had possession got,
> But "Wombwell" jealous of his neighbour king,
> Bought all his force, and formed a barrier ring.
> Determined fully to monopolise
> The little spot which Hales appeared to prize!

Hales then fought off Wombwell's men, and the ode continues;

> Hales kept possession! and the papers say,
> His prowess gained some scores of pounds that day!

Having proved a success in shows throughout England, Hales went to

Tomb of the Norfolk Giant, West Somerton.

America in 1848 on a tour arranged by the American Museum of New York. In Philadelphia, he was seen by 28,000 people in two weeks!

Hales wasn't a freak. One newspaper reported 'He is not like the so called Giants we have seen, who are generally ugly and repulsive guys, but on the contrary, Hales is handsome in features, symmetrical in figure, and exceedingly good tempered; added to which, his intellectual faculties are of the highest order.'

Eventually, Hales tired of the showbiz life and returned to London, and later, Sheffield, where he ran a pub. He died in November, 1863 on a visit to Great Yarmouth, which was near enough to his birthplace for him to be buried in the churchyard of the thatched St Mary's. His tomb is a sarcophagus on four feet.

While in the area, a visit to nearby East Somerton church ruins is very rewarding, (*Map Ref:* TG 481 196). An old oak tree is growing in the middle of this roofless church and is believed to have sprouted from the wooden leg of a witch buried there many years ago.

Places of Interest in the Neighbourhood
Mill in a Gatehouse (Ludham)
Hitler's Sapling (How Hill)
A Decayed Famous Priory (Bacton)

7 Little Domesday Book

Access: Public Records Office, Chancery Lane, London (on view to the public).

Norfolk, Suffolk and Essex are unique in that the 1086 Domesday survey of England includes these counties in a separate volume from the main record. This is known as the 'Little Domesday Book.'

In 1085, William the Conquerer ordered a survey of his newly acquired country to record the land wealth, ownership and tax due of every manor. The real purpose of the Domesday survey is still debated by historians, but the sheer volume of data collected is staggering, considering it took just one year! The Little Domesday Book reveals the date of the survey as 1086.

In most cases the record for each landholder from the king downwards shows the manorial values for 1066 and 1086 (respectively, the years of the Conquest and the survey). Also included are the persons on the estate; tenants, sub-tenants, freemen, sokemen, peasants, slaves and often resources such as mills, ponds, ploughteams and livestock. In the case of East Anglia, such detail shows it was the most populated part of the kingdom. But why are there two volumes?

The main Domesday Book is a final draft, written by just one scribe, of all the information collected in England, excluding East Anglia. The Little Domesday Book however, comprises the returns which have not been summarized. Secondly, because East Anglia was so densely populated, the data was simply too great in quantity to be tackled quickly for it contains far more detail than that in the main text. Imagine the enormous task of visiting every landholder and recording all those facts! By the time the job was done, William was dead and the desire to condense the records vanished with him.

8 Two Towered Abbey

Position: Wymondham, Norfolk.
OS Map: Thetford and Breckland, Sheet 144, 1:50,000.
Map Ref: TG 106 015.
Access: From Wymondham market place, turn down Church Street, to Becketswell Road.

Wymondham Abbey is an impressive and imposing edifice, curious for its two towers, the reasons for which are quite complex.

Founded in 1107 by William d'Albini, the church was intended for use by the monks of the abbey and also by the parishioners of Wymondham; each religious establishment being quite separate and independent of the other. This division led to hundreds of years of argument over who should use which part of the church and when.

The disputes came to a climax in 1249 and the Pope was asked to find a solution. It was agreed to divide the church; the parishioners got the nave, north aisle and the north-west tower; the monks got the rest,

Wymondham Abbey.

including a central tower (no longer standing). However, the in-fighting continued.

In the 14th century, the monks' central tower was declared unsafe and a new one was erected (this is the present, ruined octagonal tower). The monks then had the audacity to move the church bells from the parish tower into their new tower and walled off both the tower and the altar from the citizens of Wymondham. Riots against the monks ensued.

The parishioners, not to be outdone by their antagonists, raised the cash for their new, and higher, west tower (the present one). In 1448, they won the right to install their own bells which they could ring to the annoyance of the meditating monks! Life after that was comparatively peaceful and Wymondham Abbey was left with its marvellous two towers.

Places of Interest in the Neighbourhood
Kett's Oak (Wymondham)
Withburga's Spring (East Dereham)
Curious Clock Tower (Little Ellingham)

The four hundred year old oak at Wymondham.

9 Kett's Oak

Position: Wymondham, Norfolk.
OS Map: Thetford and Breckland, Sheet 144, 1:50,000.
Map Ref: TG 138 036.
Access: Between Wymondham and Hethersett on the B1172. It is marked 'Kett's Oak'.

Standing halfway between Wymondham and Hethersett is a 400 year old oak tree, bound in iron straps and propped up with large wooden supports. Its leaves are rather smaller than one would expect, probably a result of old age or decades of car fumes. It is closely associated with the life of Robert Kett of Wymondham.

Kett's Oak is reputed to have been the spot where Robert Kett, leader of the 1549 Kett Rebellion in Norfolk, made a morale-boosting speech to his followers before marching on Norwich. The Norfolk Rebellion was just a part of a nationwide revolt against enclosures of common land by landowners, high inflation and three successive bad harvests.

Kett, and his brother William, took on the leadership of the Rebellion but did not initiate it. They marched their large band of discontented followers into Norwich and camped on Mousehold Heath. The sheriff, Edmund Wyndham, declared the protesters rebels. Soon after, the rebels captured the city with much loss of life.

Armed with 12,000 troops, the Earl of Warwick attacked Kett, retook Norwich and captured the Kett brothers. They were both hanged on 7th December, 1549; Robert from Norwich Castle, William from the tower of Wymondham Abbey. Francis Blomefield, the 18th century historian, described the event thus; 'Robert Kett . . . was carried to the castle, had chains put on him, and a rope being fixed about his neck, was drawn alive from the ground, up to the gibbet, placed upon the top of the castle, and there left hanging, in remembrance of his villany, till his body, being consumed, at last fell down'.

400 years later, the people of Norwich honoured Kett as a 'notable and courageous leader in the long struggle of the common people of England to escape from a servile life into the freedom of just condition.' A plaque was placed at the site of his execution.

Places of Interest in the Neighbourhood
Two Towered Abbey (Wymondham)
Curious Clock Tower (Little Ellingham)
Withburga's Spring (East Dereham)

10 Nosey Parker

Position: Norwich, Norfolk.
OS Map: Norwich and the Broads, Sheet 134, 1:50,000.
Map Ref: TG 232 092.
Access: St Clement's is on the corner of Colegate and Fye Bridge Street.

Buried in the churchyard of St Clement's Church, Norwich, is the tomb of the parents of Archbishop Matthew Parker. It is their son whose name is associated with a most curious phrase.

Matthew Parker was born in Norwich on 6th August, 1504, and was educated at Norwich Grammar School. He was ordained and became chaplin to Anne Boleyn and Henry VIII. During Kett's Rebellion of 1549, Parker tried unsuccessfully to calm the rebels down and was lucky to escape alive, considering their anger towards the 'establishment'. In 1559, he was appointed Archbishop of Canterbury in Elizabeth I's England.

In his new post, Parker, as a fanatical Protestant, set about clarifying the principles of the Anglican Church. He was particularly fastidious at delving into the affairs of others, especially the conduct of the clergy, and he made many successful clean-up operations of ecclesiastical establishments.

He died in 1575, and his continuously curious, inquisitive nature is the origin of the useful phrase 'Nosey Parker'!

Places of Interest in the Neighbourhood
Side Saddle Introduced (Norwich)
First English Authoress (Norwich)
A Medieval Tower (Norwich)

11 Withburga's Spring

Position: East Dereham, Norfolk.
OS Map: North West Norfolk, Sheet 132, 1:50,000.
Map Ref: TF 987 134.
Access: Just off the market place in the centre of town.

St Nicholas' church, East Dereham, contains the site of a healing well over a spring which appeared at the removal of St Withburga's remains from that spot in AD974.

St Withburga was the daughter of King Anna of the East Angles (635-654), and sister of St Etheldreda, abbess and foundress of Ely. Withburga was probably educated at Holkham and, following the death of her father in 654 at the Battle of Blythburgh against King Penda, she founded a nunnery at Dereham in the same year.

Circumstances surrounding Withburga and the nunnery gave rise to her saintly disposition. Miracles occurred during her lifetime and she was buried in the churchyard at Dereham where the locals thereafter regarded her as their saint.

Legend tells us that the abbot of the cathedral at Ely, who happened to have been Dereham's overlord, wanted St Withburga's remains removed to Ely to lie in honour next to those of her sister St Etheldreda. In 974, abbot Brithnoth decided that the time had come to reunite the

St Withburga's healing well.

holy pair. This would greatly improve morale at the abbey as Ely had suffered from Danish attack and was eager to restore its standing in the Christian hierarchy.

Brithnoth organised a visit to Dereham, supposedly on a legal matter. A lavish party was held towards the end of the day and, just as the people of Dereham were recovering from the effects of the celebrations, Brithnoth and his monks put into action a daring scheme.

Under cover of darkness the Ely gang removed St Withburga's coffin from the church into which it had been moved some years previously. Hurriedly, the coffin was shifted to the river on its journey to Ely cathedral.

Wild excitement gripped the people of Dereham the following morning when they discovered the deception. Armed to the teeth, they set off after Brithnoth and their saint. On coming to the river the band divided into two groups, each on either bank. Brithnoth was sighted but the pursuers were only able to shout abuse and threats at them from the riverbank. Soon they tired, gave up and went home. The monks sailed on and managed to land at Tidbrithseie where a hearse was waiting to speed the coffin to Ely amid great rejoicing.

Places of Interest in the Neighbourhood
Two Towered Abbey (Wymondham)
Kett's Oak (Wymondham)
Curious Clock Tower (Little Ellingham)

An engraving showing survivors being rescued from the the water following the collapse of the Great Yarmouth suspension bridge in 1845.

12 A Clown and a Collapsed Bridge

Position: Great Yarmouth, Norfolk.
OS Map: Norwich and the Broads, Sheet 134, 1:50,000.
Map Ref: TG 525 081.
Access: St Nicholas' is on Priory Plain. (Tombstone lies to the right through the entrance gate).

Joseph John Scoles, church builder, also built a suspension bridge over the River Bure at Great Yarmouth which collapsed tragically in 1845.

Buried in the churchyard of St Nicholas' at Great Yarmouth lies one of the victims of that great disaster, George H J Beloe. His gravestone shows a relief of the disaster and the following inscription;

Sacred to the memory of George H J Beloe, the beloved son of Louisa Beloe, who was unfortunately drowned by the fall of the suspension bridge on 2nd May, 1845, aged 9 years.

This is indeed one of the saddest of Norfolk's many gravestones. George Beloe was one of nearly eighty lives lost that late afternoon by what now seems a ridiculous spectacle.

A clown named Nelson had caused a great crowd of between four and five hundred to gather on the bridge. Mostly women and children, they were to watch the clown sail up the Bure in a washing tub, towed by four geese! As the entertainer passed under the bridge, the crowd moved across to the other side to watch the emerging stuntman. The pressure on the chains caused them to snap and the bridge and spectators plummeted into the river below.

Many lives were saved by onlookers and people in small boats, but it was a great tragedy at the time and Nelson the clown was said never to have recovered from the shock.

St Nicholas' church is interesting in itself, being the largest parish church in England. Bombed during the last war, it was carefully restored in the late 1950s.

Places of Interest in the Neighbourhood
Nelson's Other Column (Great Yarmouth)
Tower of Cubes (Burgh St Peter)
Saxon Shore Roman Fort (Burgh Castle)

13 Hitler's Sapling

Position: How Hill, North West of Ludham, Norfolk.
OS Map: Norwich and the Broads, Sheet 134, 1:50,000.
Map Ref: TG 373 191.
Access: Follow signs to How Hill from Ludham, enter How Hill car park just before the windmill.

How Hill, with its house, marshman's 'Toad Hole' cottage and Broadland landscape alongside the River Ant, is well worth a visit. Such a collection of delights is not marred by the presence of an evil dictator's 60-year old oak tree, which begs explanation.

The Boardman family, who originally owned the property, had a keen sailor amongst its members; Christopher Boardman. He had an early career in the navy having spent much of his childhood sailing on the nearby Broads.

In 1934, Christopher Boardman made an attempt to win the America's Cup for England in his yacht *Endeavour II*. Still seeking excitement and a challenge two years later, he took *Lalage* to Nazi Germany to compete in the 1936 Berlin Olympics, overseen by the dictator Hitler himself. Competing with eleven other nations, Boardman and his team won the gold medal for Britain (which turned out to have been made almost entirely of metal!).

As part of the Olympic ceremony, Hitler awarded to each winner an oak sapling which proved, in this case, to prosper better than the prize-giver. On 20th September, 1936, the sapling was planted at How Hill and thus became known as Hitler's Oak.

A bronze plaque with the gift says 'Wachse zur Ehre des Sieges, rufe zu weiterer Tat', which, in true Nazi style, is intended to encourage one to grow in honour of victory and seek further grand feats. The tree stands just next to the house car park.

Places of Interest in the Neighbourhood
Mill in a Gatehouse (Ludham)
Norfolk Giant (West Somerton)
A Decayed Famous Priory (Bacton)

14 A Medieval Tower

Position: Norwich, Norfolk.
OS Map: Norwich and the Broads, Sheet 134, 1:50,000.
Map Ref: TG 237 077.
Access: From Carrow Hill, near Carrow Bridge.

Norwich is proud to display the bold remnants of its 13th century medieval walled fortifications. Stretching for over two miles at an average height of 6 metres (20 feet), segments of the wall and its towers present an impressive sight. The fortification shown here is part of a section running virtually intact from the River Wensum at Carrow Bridge to the arched walls on Carrow Hill. It comprises a fair length of wall with four towers close together guarding a steep approach to the city. Fortunately, this important historical relic is now protected and preserved.

   Like the City of London and Great Yarmouth, Norwich was hemmed in by its ancient walls. These enclosed about one square mile of tightly packed housing. On the eastern boundary the river naturally forms part of this defence. Two medieval gateways, at King Street and Ber Street, formed either end of this part of the city fortification.

   Starting at the Wensum, a path called 'Way under the Walls' leads up

Black Tower, part of the medieval defences of Norwich.

to the two towers on Carrow Hill. Looking back to the river, two 'boom' towers can be seen. A chain was suspended between these outposts to control river traffic. The King Street boom tower housed the winch which lifted the chain high enough to allow boats through. Access to the opposite boom tower is across the bridge and along the Riverside Walk.

Following the arrow-slitted wall up Carrow Hill, one comes upon Wilderness Tower. This monster guarded the lower slopes and is about 6 metres (20 feet) high. A view of its interior can be had through the iron gate in its base.

The higher, larger and better preserved Black Tower, so called because of its black flints, stands defiantly at the top of the slope. Arrow slits and windows can be seen and there is a doorway into it from the upper ramparts. In 1665-6, Black Tower was used as a detention centre for Plague victims.

Much has been done this century to rid the walls of plant growth and substantial remains have been made accessible. Tracing the full extent of this defensive bastion can prove exhausting, and it ends on the other side of the city at the 15 metre (50 feet) Cow Tower near Bishop Bridge.

Places of Interest in the Neighbourhood
First English Authoress (Norwich)
Side Saddle Introduced (Norwich)
Nosey Parker (Norwich)

15 Side Saddle Introduced

Position: St Andrew's Hill, Norwich.
OS Map: Norwich and the Broads, Sheet 134, 1:50,000.
Map Ref: TG 231 087.
Access: St Andrew's church lies on the corner of St Andrew's Hill and St Andrew's Street.

King Richard II was married to Anne, daughter of the Holy Roman Emperor Charles IV and sister of King Wenceslas of Bohemia. Francis Blomefield, the respected 18th century historian, described their royal visit to Norwich in 1383; '. . . he was received here with great pomp, for in the city accounts there are many sums paid for new painting of the city banner, fitting up and painting their admiral's barge, etc., and putting up all the city furniture in order for that purpose.'

Queen Anne made a great and lasting impact on Norfolk life in particular and national horseriding in general. It was she who introduced a new style of riding, as Blomefield relates so well; '. . . the English ladies, after the example of Queen Anne, daughter to the King of Bohemia, and wife to King Richard, began to ride on side saddles; this Queen first brought this fashion into the land, for before, women used to ride astride like men.'

Her visit is commemorated by the inclusion in a frieze of shields on the southern side of St Andrew's church, Norwich, of the coat-of-arms of the Holy Roman Emperor; the double-headed eagle.

Places of Interest in the Neighbourhood
Nosey Parker (Norwich)
First English Authoress (Norwich)
A Medieval Tower (Norwich)

16 The Oldest Man-Made Norfolk Curiosity

Position: 5km/3m East of Weeting, Norfolk.
OS Map: Thetford and Breckland, Sheet 144, 1:50,000.
Map Ref: TL 817 899.
Access: Off the A134 Thetford – Mundford road. (Open to the public).

Covering 34 acres and lying beneath the heath of Breckland are the fascinating prehistoric flint mines known as Grime's Graves. Neolithic miners are believed to have started work there about 10,000BC, reaching a peak around 2000BC and finishing near 500BC. The site was a massive, industrious enterprise. Flint was removed from the chalk either in opencast mines or from pits dug deep into the ground, evidence of which can still be seen. Long tunnels connected many of these shafts. Archaeologists have unearthed thousands of antler picks, one with a Neolithic finger print. Early man used the flint for making into cutting tools, axes, arrow and spear heads.

Early studies of Grime's Graves showed them to have been fortifications or dwellings. The 1586 Camden *Britannia* stated, 'At a mile's distance eastward of Weeting is a hill with certain small trenches of ancient fortifications called Grime's Graves, of which name the inhabitants can give no account.' Later, in the 18th century, the historian Frances Blomefield described the area as 'a very curious Danish Encampment.'

It was not until 1869 that the true nature of Grime's Graves was revealed, (Anglo-Saxon 'Graves' means 'holes' or 'hollows'). The Reverend Canon Greenwell carried out some investigations into this rare ancient site and discovered it was indeed an extensive network of mines.

Places of Interest in the Neighbourhood
Buried Treasure (Swaffham)
Pingo Ponds (Thompson)
Where Three Parishes Meet (Elveden)

17 Nelson's Other Column

Position: Great Yarmouth, Norfolk,
OS Map: Norwich and the Broads, Sheet 134, 1:50,000.
Map Ref: TG 529 055.
Access: Monument Road, South Denes. (Column open July and August).

Horatio Nelson, the most famous English naval hero, was born in Burnham Thorpe in Norfolk, and it was considered fitting that a monument to him be erected at Great Yarmouth in 1817.

Nelson's Column at Great Yarmouth.

The fluted Athenian Doric column stands in South Denes topped with the figure of Britannia ruling the waves. It is 43 metres (144 feet) high, based on the Monument to the fire of London, and is 20 years earlier than the famous Nelson's column in Trafalgar Square. Inscribed at the base are Nelson's victories; Aboukir, St Vincent, Copenhagen, Trafalgar.

The curiosity behind the column lies with Britannia. Why does she face inland and not out to sea as one would expect in a naval monument? There are two plausible explanations; she faces Nelson's birthplace; she faces the river port where Yarmouth's prosperity was generated and highlights its important sea-going connections. Life for the monument began with an unfortunate incident.

There is an interior staircase which in 1819, just prior to its opening, was climbed by the city's chief surveyor and the first Yarmouth librarian, Thomas Sutton, who collapsed and died of exhaustion at the attempt.

Places of Interest in the Neighbourhood
A Clown and a Collapsed Bridge (Great Yarmouth)
Tower of Cubes (Burgh St Peter)
Saxon Shore Roman Fort (Burgh Castle)

The neo-classical mausoleum of John Hobart.

18 Pyramid Mausoleum

Position: Blickling Hall, Norfolk.
OS Map: North East Norfolk, Sheet 133, 1:50,000.
Map Ref: TG 166 295.
Access: Near Aylsham, turn off the B1354 Aylsham-Saxthorpe road towards Itteringham Common. Car park on corner near 'Great Wood'.

Lying in the grounds of the marvellous Blickling Hall, now owned by the National Trust, is a stark, neo-classical pyramid containing the remains of John Hobart, 2nd Earl of Buckinghamshire, who lived at the Hall.

John Hobart was the grandson of Henry Hobart, killed in a duel in 1698 (see 'Duel to the Death'). He became Earl in 1756; Ambassador to St Petersburg between 1762 and 1765; and, Lord Lieutenant of Ireland 1777-80. In 1793, Lord Buckinghamshire died under mysterious circumstances. The Blickling Hall guidebook quotes Horace Walpole as saying that Lord Buckinghamshire 'suffered from gout in his foot, dipped it in cold water, and so killed himself.'

During his lifetime, he made fashionable alterations to Blickling, employing the skills of the Ivory family (Thomas Ivory built the Assembly Room in Norwich). Beginning in 1761, his modernisations included; the enchanting Chinese Bedroom with its hand-painted wallpaper; his Peter the Great Room (named after its Russian tapestry of the Tsar); and, the obviously neo-classical State Bedroom. A visit to Blickling is not complete without seeing both Hall and gardens (open to the public).

Also nearby, and marked 'Tower' on the map, is an unusual embattled brick house and tower (TG 161 288).

Places of Interest in the Neighbourhood
Duel to the Death (Cawston)
The Moved Church (Edgefield)
A Decayed Famous Priory (Bacton)

19 Curious Clock Tower

Position: Little Ellingham, Norfolk.
OS Map: Thetford and Breckland, Sheet 144, 1:50,000.
Map Ref: TM 003 995.
Access: Near The Green, just inside the entrance to the Hall.

Standing in the grounds of the Hall at Little Ellingham is this tall clock
tower with four cottages at its base. The four houses are joined in a
cross shape and the whole Italian style construction is very attractive
despite the obvious decay to the clocks.

   Built in 1855, the same year as the Hall, the dwellings were for the
benefit of the estate gardeners who, presumably, were never late for
work or meals!

Places of Interest in the Neighbourhood
Pingo Ponds (Thompson)
Two Towered Abbey (Wymondham)
Kett's Oak (Wymondham)

Little Ellingham clock tower.

20 The Moved Church

Position: Edgefield, Norfolk.
OS Map: North East Norfolk, Sheet 133, 1:50,000.
Map Ref: TG 093 343.
Access: Off the B1149 Saxthorpe-Holt road.

Canon Walter Herbert Marcon was a remarkable man for at least two
reasons; he was rector of St Peter and St Paul, Edgefield for a total of 63
years from 1875 to 1937; and, he moved the original church half a mile
to its present position!

   Canon Marcon was born in 1850 at Edgefield rectory and actually
died in the same room in 1937. On taking up the post of rector, Marcon
found the church dilapidated and badly sited. The Black Death of 1349
had caused the people of Edgefield to move away from around the
church and the valley in which they lived. They settled on higher
ground.

   When Marcon took over he planned the unusual task of dismantling
and reassembling the church in the centre of the village as it was then.

The church of St Peter and St Paul, Edgefield.

Architect J D Sedding had surveyed the old church in 1876 and recorded serious decay. He arranged the construction of the new building and Marcon raised the money required. The job of rebuilding took ten years, though the actual reconstruction took just two years from 1883-85. Marcon wrote; 'Bit by bit the roofs were taken down, the walls slowly razed to the ground – all the wrought stones were marked so as to ensure each stone going into its proper place.'

A new tower was built 1907-9, and in 1921 a First World War memorial clock was added as a tribute to the local dead.

At the original site just the 13th century octagonal tower is left standing in Glaven Valley (TG 086 346). Nearby there is an artificial mound built during the time of the Armada as a base for a warning beacon. (The old tower is located by turning left at the present church gate, then second right at the crossroads towards Hunworth, and it's on the left about half a mile).

Places of Interest in the Neighbourhood
Pyramid Mausoleum (Blickling)
Duel to the Death (Cawston)
A Decayed Famous Priory (Bacton)

The Swaffham town sign showing the Pedlar.

21 Buried Treasure

Position: Swaffham, Norfolk.
OS Map: Thetford and Breckland, Sheet 144, 1:50,000.
Map Ref: TF 821 089.
Access: Swaffham church lies in the centre of town.

A mixture of fact and fiction has created the curious tale of how John Chapman, 'Pedlar of Swaffham', became very rich.

Around the middle of the 15th century, Chapman told his wife Catherine about a recurring dream. In this dream Chapman was told to go to London Bridge and there he would find his fortune! Being a pedlar or tinker by trade Chapman must have seen in this an opportunity, and he duly went off on foot to the capital.

On the bridge Chapman met a total stranger who had also had a dream which he related to the Swaffham pedlar. The stranger told Chapman that he'd dreamt about a pot of gold which was buried under a fruit tree in the garden of a pedlar in Swaffham!

Needless to say, Chapman dashed back home, dug deep beneath his apple tree and there found a pot of gold with the inscription;

> Under me doth lie,
> Another richer than I.

And the pedlar dug even deeper and found a second, larger pot full of gold.

The facts show that John Chapman was made Church Warden in 1462, and that he must have been respected by the people of Swaffham. The church was in a poor state due to the collapse of the tower in 1454, which caused considerable damage. A programme of restoration and rebuilding was started. On his appointment Chapman payed enough gold to build a new north aisle and part of the replacement tower.

Perhaps Chapman did find gold as the tale reveals. Or maybe the story covers up some illicit gold smuggling which Chapman, as a traveller, may have come across. Either way, Swaffham celebrates this legend with the pedlar's image upon its town sign.

Places of Interest in the Neighbourhood
The Oldest Man-Made Norfolk Curiosity (Grime's Graves)
Pingo Ponds (Thompson)
Curious Clock Tower (Little Ellingham)

22 Tower of Cubes

Position: Burgh St Peter, Norfolk.
OS Map: Norwich and the Broads, Sheet 134, 1:50,000.
Map Ref: TM 493 937.
Access: Off the A143 Yarmouth-Bungay road. At Haddiscoe, take the road to Burgh St Peter and continue on to Staithe.

Towering above the desolate marshes, at the end of a long track from Haddiscoe, is one of England's most extraordinary and curious towers. Made of brick, it has variously been referred to as 'a folly', 'a monstrosity' and 'a pyramid', as it is a pile of giant cubes carefully balanced one on top of the other, and growing smaller as they go up.

One explanation for the unusual shape could be that the surrounding land being marshy would not hold a conventional tower. Its base, however, is part of the original 16th century tower which did fall down.

St Mary's tower serves as a memorial or mausoleum to Samuel Boycott who built it in 1793 as a replacement for the earlier tower destroyed in a storm, and he lies buried beneath it. The Boycott's were rectors of St Mary's from 1764 to 1899, and there are brass memorials to the family within this delightful thatched church on the River Waveney with Suffolk on the opposite bank.

Places of Interest in the Neighbourhood
Nelson's Other Column (Great Yarmouth)
A Clown and a Collapsed Bridge (Great Yarmouth)
Saxon Shore Roman Fort (Burgh Castle)

, One of England's most extraordinary church towers.

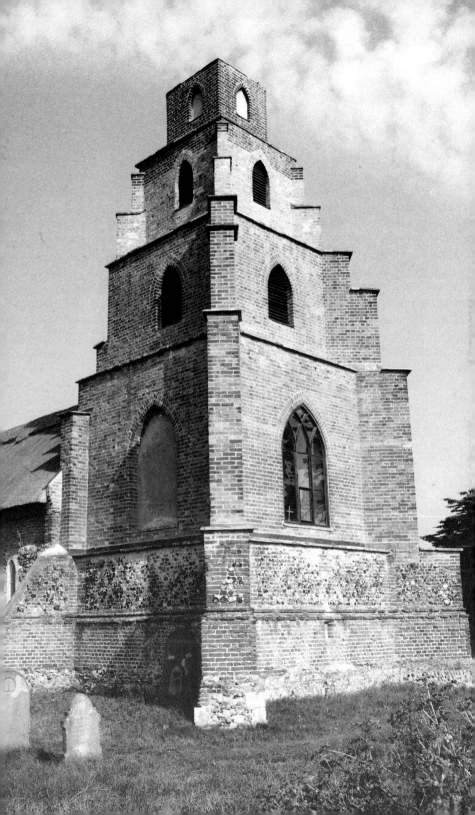

23 The Shattered Maid's Heart

Position: Tuesday Market Place, King's Lynn, Norfolk.
OS Map: North West Norfolk, Sheet 132, 1:50,000.
Map Ref: TF 617 204.
Access: The Tuesday Market Place is towards the northern end of the town.

A fascinating and gruesome tale surrounds the origin of the carving of a heart located in the Tuesday Market Place in King's Lynn. This prosperous port had, like so many other European towns, a most horrid way of dealing with certain criminals: boiling to the death. Such displays in Lynn's market place were sure crowd-pullers in 16th century England.

The popularity of boiling to the death reached a peak in 1531 with the introduction of an Act specifically dealing with poisoners and which legalised the use of the cauldron as a means of execution.

That year a maid servant was extremely unfortunate both to have poisoned her mistress and to get caught. She was duly sentenced, though her act may well have been a simple case of food poisoning misunderstood by a superstitious people; nobody now knows.

Taken in chains to the market place, she was suspended above a giant boiling cauldron over an enormous fire. At the very moment that the water boiled, the terrified maid was lowered into the cauldron, raised and lowered again and again, as was the general practice. Amazingly, the water being so scalding, the girl's chest burst open and her heart was propelled across the market place, hitting the wall on the other side. There today, you can see the spot marked with a carving of a heart in a diamond, (on the wall of a house at the narrow end of the market place).

Places of Interest in the Neighbourhood
Haunted by a Fiddler (King's Lynn)
Detached Church Tower (West Walton)
Killed by a Pinprick (Stow Bartolph)

The heart in a diamond, Tuesday Market Place, King's Lynn.

24 Haunted by a Fiddler

Position: St James' Park, King's Lynn, Norfolk.
OS Map: North West Norfolk, Sheet 132, 1:50,000.
Map Ref: TF 625 198.
Access: Red Mount Chapel is on a mound on 'The Walks' in the park.

Red Mount Chapel is a superb example of the Gothic style in architecture and even boasts its own musical ghost!

Built in 1485 at the time of Henry VII – the first Tudor king, it was a stopping-off place for pilgrims on their way to Walsingham via the port of King's Lynn. Octagonal in shape, it is very small, and has three floors. The top floor is a chapel with fan tracery much like that in Cambridge's King's College.

Underneath the chapel building there is reputed to be a long tunnel (not unusual), running to Castle Rising – a distance of 18km/12 miles (very unusual). An unfortunate, drunken fiddler once decided to explore the dark passageway with his instrument, his dog and his pint! He never reached the end of the tunnel, wherever it went, but his spirit remains and can be heard on occasions playing his tunes and singing, accompanied by the whining of his poor dog!

Places of Interest in the Neighbourhood
The Shattered Maid's Heart (King's Lynn)
Killed by a Pinprick (Stow Bartolph)
Detached Church Tower (West Walton)

Red Mount Chapel.

25 Detached Church Tower

Position: West Walton, Norfolk.
OS Map: Ely and Wisbech, Sheet 143, 1:50,000.
Map Ref: TF 471 133.
Access: Off the A47 Wisbech-King's Lynn road. St Mary's is in the centre of the village.

St Mary's, West Walton, is unusual in that its tower is completely detached from the church. It is a magnificent structure in the Early English style of the 13th century. Constructed in Barnack stone, the

Detached church tower at West Walton.

tower stands on four great arches, remarkably so, considering that the ground is potentially swampy in this remote, westerly part of Norfolk. This may have been the reason for its detachment – in case of subsidence and possible damage to the church. However, there it stands, proud and solid.

As usual with many interesting historical buildings there is a tale which offers its own explanation as to the reason for a separate tower. Legend tells us that the Devil, assisted by some wicked fenmen, tried to remove the tower but only managed to carry it a few feet from the church.

Inside the church there is a record of disasters passed, but ever present; 'On ye 1st November, 1613, the sea broke in and overflowed all Marshland to the great danger of Mens lives and losse of goods. On the 23rd March, 1614, this country was overflowed with the fresh (water). And on the 12th and 13th September, 1671, all Marshland was againe overflowed by the Violence of the Sea.'

Places of Interest in the Neighbourhood
Haunted by a Fiddler (King's Lynn)
The Shattered Maid's Heart (King's Lynn)
Killed by a Pinprick (Stow Bartolph)

26 Killed by a Pinprick

Position: Stow Bartolph, Norfolk,
OS Map: Ely and Wisbech, Sheet 143, 1:50,000.
Map Ref: TF 629 057.
Access: Just off the A10 Downham Market-King's Lynn road.

Sarah Hare of Stow Bartolph was punished for working on Sunday.
Back in 1744, she ignored the conventions of the Sabbath and decided
to do some sewing. Whether it was Divine intervention or sheer lack of
concentration, Sarah pricked her finger with a pin and died as a result.

Before she passed away she ordered that her memory be not forgot-
ten. A wax, life-size and life-like model of her was made, dressed and
mounted in a wall cabinet of the Holy Trinity Church at Stow Bartolph.
There it remains, staring awesomely and hauntingly real.

Places of Interest in the Neighbourhood
Detached Church Tower (West Walton)
Haunted by a Fiddler (King's Lynn)
The Shattered Maid's Heart (King's Lynn)

The wax figure of Sarah Hare of Stow Bartolph.

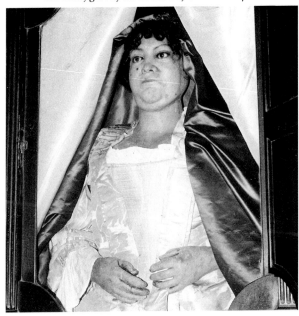

27 Saxon Shore Roman Fort

Position: Burgh Castle, Norfolk.
OS Map: Norwich and the Broads, Sheet 134, 1:50,000.
Map Ref: TG 474 045.
Access: Turn off the A143 Bungay-Great Yarmouth road near Belton. Park at church and follow signs to the fort.

This three-sided rectangular fort represented one of ancient Rome's distant stands against invading Saxons. It is greatly admired, if only because so much of it remains.

Burgh Castle was one of the ten defensive fortresses built on England's east and south-east coasts in the 3rd century AD. In those days, 'Gariannonum', as it was known, was a Roman town and port on a huge estuary, while Great Yarmouth was only a sand bank. The sea has since receded and Yarmouth was created in the process. Also nearby were the Roman towns of Caister and Venta Incenorum near Norwich. These were separated from Burgh Castle by a vast but shallow estuary.

Burgh Castle now lies above the River Waveney where there are three surviving walls of about 4·5 metres (15 feet) in height. At each corner large bastions have been added.

Cavalry troops would have been stationed here ready to repel Saxon invaders from the sea. Flaming beacons would have been used to signal such an attack. Soon, the call to defend Rome itself caused Burgh to be deserted to the Saxons who settled here in strength.

In the 7th century, King Sigebert of the East Angles gave Burgh Castle to Saint Fursey who came from Ireland in 633. He set up a monastery here as part of a process of converting the Saxons to Christianity.

In their turn, the Normans erected a motte and bailey castle within the Roman walls as part of their complete takeover of England. This was thought to have been built by Ralph the Engineer who owned the site at the time of the Domesday survey in 1086. The importance of Burgh Castle as a defensive stronghold soon diminished however, and the whole edifice was left to decay.

Places of Interest in the Neighbourhood
 A Clown and a Collapsed Bridge (Great Yarmouth)
Nelson's Other Column (Great Yarmouth)
Tower of Cubes (Burgh St Peter)

The Roman fort at Burgh Castle.

28 Where Three Parishes Meet

Position: Elveden, Suffolk.
OS Map: Thetford, Breckland and surrounding area, Sheet 144,
1:50,000.
Map Ref: TL 788 776.
Access: On the A11, 10km/6m SW of Thetford, marked on the map as
'Mon'.

The Elveden Memorial serves as a distinctive landmark for travellers
between Newmarket and Norwich. Its grand Corinthian column,
capped with an urn, stands to a height of 30 metres (100 feet), and
is beautifully proportioned. Interestingly, it is sighted where three
parishes meet; Elveden, Eriswell and Icklingham.

   Designed by Clyde Young, it was erected in 1921 and dedicated to the
memory of the local soldiers from each of the three parishes who died in
the First World War. Their names have been immortalised on the base.
This list is much longer than that added following the Second World
War, probably reflecting a decline in the rural population between the
wars.

Places of Interest in the Neighbourhood
Pingo Ponds (Thompson)
The Oldest Man-Made Norfolk Curiosity (Grime's Graves)
A Gypsy Grave (Moulton)

(for illustration see frontispiece)

29 A Gypsy Grave

Position: Moulton, Suffolk.
OS Map: Cambridge, Newmarket and surrounding area, Sheet 154, 1:50,000.
Map Ref: TL 687 661.
Access: At the crossroads of the Chippenham-Moulton and Newmarket-Kentford (B1506) roads.

It is always tragic when youth dies needlessly. Attached to one such death is a tale of great mystery. This concerns an unfortunate shepherd called Joseph the Gypsy Boy, for he lies buried at the side of a road just outside Moulton.

The tale relates that sometime in the early 19th century Joseph was tending his sheep near this spot when one of the flock went missing. Joseph was accused of stealing the sheep and, knowing that the penalty for such a crime was death, he became very distraught and hanged himself. As suicides were refused burial in the churchyard, Joseph was quickly interred at this roadside spot.

Locals still strongly believe in this tale and the mystery continues as the grave is regularly tended, with fresh flowers carefully set up by unknown visitors and well-wishers.

Places of Interest in the Neighbourhood
Where Three Parishes Meet (Elveden)
A Bishop's Fantasy (Horringer)

The grave of Joseph, the Gypsy Boy.

30 Book Bound With Murderer's Skin

Position: Moyse's Hall Museum, Bury St Edmunds, Suffolk.
OS Map: Bury St Edmunds and Sudbury area, Sheet 155, 1:50,000.
Map Ref: TL 853 644.
Access: On the corner of Buttermarket and Brentgovel Street, (open to the public, entrance free).

In Moyse's Hall Museum in Bury St Edmunds there is a gruesome collection of artefacts connected with a murder in Victorian Suffolk. Included among these are the murder weapon, the death mask of the murderer, his scalp and ear, and a book bound with the murderer's skin. Such objects are preserved because of the intense public interest in the crime and everything connected with it.

Local girl Maria Marten was murdered by farmer William Corder on 18th May, 1827. He shot and stabbed her in the head at the Red Barn in Polstead. The two had been having an affair and had fallen out with each other.

An unusual occurrence led to the discovery of Maria's body a year after her death. Her stepmother dreamt that her body lay in the Red Barn and, on investigating, Maria's father discovered the body in that place. Corder was arrested in London and tried at Bury. Public interest was immense, and Corder was found guilty and hanged, watched by about 20,000 people.

After the execution, his body went on show at the Shire Hall and the hangman sold off pieces of the rope for souvenirs. As if this was not enough for Corder's body, it passed to the local hospital for dissection in front of students, and his skeleton was used at West Suffolk Hospital for anatomy instruction until just after the last war.

Places of Interest in the Neighbourhood
The Smallest Pub (Bury St Edmunds)
Memorials to Unfortunates (Bury St Edmunds)
Floating Turtle Clock (Bury St Edmunds)
Old Plague Stone (Bury St Edmunds)

31 The Smallest Pub

Position: Bury St Edmunds, Suffolk.
OS Map: Bury St Edmunds and Sudbury area, Sheet 155, 1:50,000.
Map Ref: TL 853 638.
Access: On the corner of Whiting Street and Westgate Street, Bury St Edmunds.

England's smallest pub, whose one bar measures only just over 5 metres by 2 metres (16'x7'), can be found in Bury, and is appropriately called 'The Nutshell'. It has stood on this corner for many years but has not always been a pub. In 1820 it was used as a fruiterers.

Inside, there are old wooden seats and panels with curios dangling from the ceiling, including the mummified remains of a cat. Perhaps this is to prove that there is just about enough room to swing one!

Places of Interest in the Neighbourhood
Book Bound with Murderer's Skin (Bury St Edmunds)
Memorials to Unfortunates (Bury St Edmunds)
Floating Turtle Clock (Bury St Edmunds)
Old Plague Stone (Bury St Edmunds)

The Nutshell Pub, England's smallest.

32 Memorials to Unfortunates

Position: Bury St Edmunds, Suffolk.
OS Map: Bury St Edmunds and Sudbury area, Sheet 155, 1:50,000.
Map Ref: TL 857 641.
Access: Off the path between Shire Hall (Honey Hill), and the Norman Tower on Crown Street.

The Charnel-House at Bury, in the splendid grounds of the old abbey, once housed the bodies of unfortunates who may have died in unusual circumstances. Testimonials to some of these are to be found on the walls of the ruinous Charnel-House where a warning to us all can be seen on a gravestone covered in carved skulls and bones;

> Sarah, wife of Edward Warton,
> died 7th November, 1698, aged 69.
> Good people all as you pass by,
> Look round see how corpses do lie,
> For as you are, sometime were we.
> And as we are so must you be.

Nine year old Mary Haselton, 'virtuously brought up', was praying on 16th August, 1785, when she was 'instantaneously killed by a flash of lightning'.

Another memorial begs to be read;

> Reader, pause at this humble stone, it records
> the tale of unguarded youth by the allurements
> of vice and the treacherous snares of seduction.
> Sarah Lloyd, on the 23rd April, 1800, in the 22nd
> year of her age, suffered a just but ignominious
> death for admitting her abandoned seducer into
> the dwelling house of her mistress in the night
> of 3rd October, 1799, and becoming the instrument
> in his hands of the crimes of robbery and house-
> burning. These were her last words:
> "May my example be a warning to thousands."

Presumably, Sarah was hanged for her part in this unfortunate affair.

Places of Interest in the Neighbourhood
Book Bound with Murderer's Skin (Bury St Edmunds)
The Smallest Pub (Bury St Edmunds)
Floating Turtle Clock (Bury St Edmunds)
Old Plague Stone (Bury St Edmunds)

The Charnel-House.

33 Floating Turtle Clock

Position: Bury St Edmunds, Suffolk.
OS Map: Bury St Edmunds and Sudbury area, Sheet 155, 1:50,000.
Map Ref: TL 857 639.
Access: On Honey Hill, opposite Court House.

Frederick Gershom Parkington was a keen collector of time pieces. These are now housed in the Manor House Museum at Bury, one of Great Britain's finest collections of clocks and watches, forming a memorial to his son John who died in the Second World War. Scattered throughout the museum are the various time measuring instruments amid furniture on loan from the Victoria and Albert Museum. Also on display are some fine and decorative art objects.

   Most curious are, to mention just a few; a wooden framed turret clock of 1692 from Stowmarket; a demonstration model of Su Sung's water clock of 1090; a fascinating working model of a revolving ball clock of 1860; Giovanni di Dondi's Planetarium Clock and Calendar of the 14th century; and, my favourite, an early 20th century replica of a 17th century clock where the time is told by a turtle floating on a dish of water!

Places of Interest in the Neighbourhood
The Smallest Pub (Bury St Edmunds)
Memorials to Unfortunates (Bury St Edmunds)
Old Plague Stone (Bury St Edmunds)

The Old Plague Stone on Out Risbygate.

34 Old Plague Stone

Position: Bury St Edmunds, Suffolk.
OS Map: Bury St Edmunds and Sudbury area, Sheet 155, 1:50,000.
Map Ref: TL 843 645.
Access: On Out Risbygate (Newmarket Road), A1302.

Standing in the grounds of the West Suffolk College at Bury St
Edmunds, and looking like the foot of a single stone column, is the Old
Plague Stone, the material of which came from Barrack Quarry in
Cambridgeshire. Indeed, it was once the base of a cross erected at the
edge of the city on Risbygate Street. Presumably, the cross became
decayed and was removed leaving the stone stump to be utilized in
desperate times as a 'plague stone'.

Placed just outside the city walls, the stone has a small font used to
hold vinegar or a spirit solution. Into this liquid the citizens of Bury, in
times of plague or disease (which were numerous in the 18th century),
would place their money for goods which were brought to the stone
by outsiders or traders from the countryside. The whole process was
intended to cut down the possibility of infection.

This interesting relic shows how distraught and desperate were the
people in attempting to combat the devastating effects of disease. Not
until the progress of science and the introduction of vaccines were the
plague stones of English towns dismantled.

Places of Interest in the Neighbourhood
Book Bound with Murderer's Skin (Bury St Edmunds)
The Smallest Pub (Bury St Edmunds)
Memorials to Unfortunates (Bury St Edmunds)
Floating Turtle Clock (Bury St Edmunds)

35 A Bishop's Fantasy

Position: Horringer, Bury St Edmunds, Suffolk.
OS Map: Bury St Edmunds and Sudbury area, Sheet 155, 1:50,000.
Map Ref: TL 816 614.
Access: Marked on the map as 'Ickworth House', just off the A143, 3km/2m SW of Bury (open to the public).

Ickworth House is famous for its wonderful fantasy rotunda, built for the eccentric 4th Earl of Bristol, Bishop of Derry, Frederick Augustus Hervey. He died without ever seeing the house completed.

Architect Francis Sandys followed Hervey's idea for Ickworth based on a similar passion at Ballyscullion. Branching off the central living area were two curved wings for the Earl's art collection purchased on the 'Grand Tours' of the Continent. Work began on the house in 1795.

In 1798, Hervey was taken prisoner in Italy by revolutionary Napoleonic forces and his art collection was confiscated. However, the Bishop was allowed to continue his tour and in 1803 he died near Albano from stomach gout.

The house was finished in about 1830 and is now gloriously maintained by the National Trust.

Places of Interest in the Neighbourhood
Old Plague Stone (Bury St Edmunds)
Book Bound with Murderer's Skin (Bury St Edmunds)
The Smallest Pub (Bury St Edmunds)
Memorials to Unfortunates (Bury St Edmunds)
Floating Turtle Clock (Bury St Edmunds)

Ickworth House.

36 Victim of the Poll Tax

Position: Sudbury, Suffolk.
OS Map: Bury St Edmunds and Sudbury area, Sheet 155, 1:50,000.
Map Ref: TL 871 415.
Access: St Gregory's Church, The Croft, Sudbury, (access to the vestry by arrangement with the rector, or verger).

Public uprisings against Poll Taxes are historically to be expected. Those of 1381 were known as the Peasant's Revolt and were particularly violent. The grimacing head of Simon Theobold, Chancellor of England in charge of Poll Tax collection, can today be seen in a glass box in the vestry of St Gregory's at Sudbury.

Simon of Sudbury was born around 1320, educated in Paris and Rome, became Bishop of London in 1362 and Archbishop of Canterbury in 1377. In that year he crowned Richard II king of England. Moving upwards in the secular field, he was appointed Chancellor in 1380; a move he would soon regret.

He introduced the Poll Tax of 1380 and, together with the Black Death and poor pay for workers, this sparked off Wat Tyler's rebellion. Each person over fifteen years of age was required to pay the new tax. Snoopers were sent around the country in search of evaders. The rebels decided to make an example of Simon and he was executed on Tower Hill, London, and his head impaled on Tower Bridge. From there, the head was transferred to Sudbury where it remains today, minus teeth which were sold off as relics. An exhibition in the church shows a photograph of the head.

Order was soon restored by the government and the rebels were crushed in a brutal manner likely to ward off similar disturbances for some time. In The Croft outside the church many rebels met their death by beheading.

Places of Interest in the Neighbourhood
An Elizabethan Conduit (Long Melford)
To See Forty Churches (Pentlow)
Soldier of Fortune (Sible Hedingham)

37 Medieval Bell-Cage

Position: East Bergholt, Suffolk.
OS Map: Bury St Edmunds and Sudbury area, Sheet 155, 1:50,000.
Map Ref: TM 070 345.
Access: St Mary's Church lies opposite the 'Old Hall' at East Bergholt.

In the village where Constable was born in 1776, lie England's heaviest church bells, secured behind the thick wooden walls of a Bell-Cage. In total, the five bells weigh just over four tons!

This unusual structure was erected in 1531 as a safe house for the bells. St Mary's church tower remained incomplete at this time due to the lack of support from its sponsor Cardinal Wolsey. The Bell-Cage was seen then as a temporary measure.

Four of the bells are of the 17th and 18th centuries with the oldest being from 1450. Each bell is housed upside down and rung by hand.

In the 17th century, local resident Joseph Chaplin found the noise of the bell ringing too much to bear so he paid to have the cage re-erected in its present position from the east side of the church. Did the same bells force Constable to seek solitude in painting in the quiet countryside of Suffolk?

Places of Interest in the Neighbourhood
The Tattingstone Wonder (Tattingstone)
Saint-Maker of Holbrook (Holbrook)
Robert Adam's Towers (Mistley)

Home of England's heaviest church bells, East Bergholt.

38 The Tattingstone Wonder

Position: Tattingstone, Suffolk.
OS Map: Ipswich and The Naze area, Sheet 169, 1:50,000.
Map Ref: TM 139 363.
Access: Marked on the map as 'Tattingstone Wonder', turn off the
A137 Colchester – Ipswich road, and it is on the shore of the Alton
Water reservoir.

Edward White lived in Tattingstone Place on the eastern side of Alton
Water. He had most of his needs there, most that is except a glimpse of
a typical English church; what better to add to the view from his house?

But Edward White was a practical man. Around 1790, he built the
'Tattingstone Wonder', and a wonder it really is. It looks just like a
church but serves as three cottages and earns income from its occupants
who pay rent.

From the road going to the A137 (past White House Farm), one can
plainly see the false tower on the look-alike church; it is only complete
as far as it can be seen from the front!

Places of Interest in the Neighbourhood
Saint-Maker of Holbrook (Holbrook)
A Tower for Study (Freston)
A Tudor Eccentricity (Erwarton)

Not really a church at all – 'The Tattingstone Wonder'.

39 Saint-Maker of Holbrook

Position: Holbrook, Suffolk.
OS Map: Ipswich and The Naze area, Sheet 169, 1:50,000.
Map Ref: TM 170 361.
Access: All Saint's Church is on the B1080 at Holbrook, off the A137 Colchester – Ipswich road.

Among the forty martyrs of England and Wales to have been canonized in 1970 was Margaret Clitherow (1556-86). Many years of deliberation and investigation are undertaken when such declarations are made and there had always been evidence of Margaret Clitherow's resistance to oppression.

She was sentenced by Judge John Clench, whose monumental effigy is in All Saint's Church, Holbrook, together with that of his wife and twelve children.

In the 16th century England of Henry VIII, it was an offence to be a practising Catholic as Margaret Clitherow was. She had mass said at her home where she was accused of harbouring priests from capture. These facts came to the attention of the authorities, who arrested her in March, 1586.

Margaret refused to plead, and the sentence passed by Judge Clench at York was one of death by crushing. On 25th March, 1586, Margaret Clitherow, 'Martyr of York', was violently compressed beneath 800 pounds, taking fifteen minutes to die.

Places of Interest in the Neighbourhood
The Tattingstone Wonder (Tattingstone)
A Tower for Study (Freston)
A Tudor Eccentricity (Erwarton)

Tomb of Judge John Clench, Holbrook.

40 A Tudor Eccentricity

Position: Erwarton, Suffolk.
OS Map: Ipswich and The Naze area, Sheet 169, 1:50,000.
Map Ref: TM 224 352.
Access: At Erwarton, marked on the map as 'Erwarton Hall' and is opposite a small pond.

Erwarton Hall gatehouse is a most amazing structure, comical, yet carefully constructed. Made around 1549 of red bricks, its vertical tubes are delightfully formed.

   Behind the gate house stands the Hall itself. Anne Boleyn is said to have stayed here and her heart was buried in the church chancel. In the early 19th century, church alterations led to the discovery of a lead casket in the shape of a heart. It was reburied under the organ.

   During the Civil War, the Hall was used as a lodging for Royalist troops who were ruthless or desperate enough to melt down the church bells for shot.

Places of Interest in the Neighbourhood
Saint-Maker of Holbrook (Holbrook)
The Tattingstone Wonder (Tattingstone)
A Tower for Study (Freston)

Erwarton gatehouse, 1549.

41 A Tower for Study

Position: Freston, Suffolk.
OS Map: Ipswich and The Naze area, Sheet 169, 1:50,000.
Map Ref: TM 177 397.
Access: Marked on the map as 'Tower', it stands in Freston Park; access by foot from the B1456 Ipswich-Shotley road.

Lord de Freston's tower, overlooking the River Orwell and designed by William Latimer, is probably England's oldest folly. It originates from the time of Henry VIII and was planned as a remote place of study for Lord de Freston's daughter Ellen. It is contemporary with Erwarton and appears to be made out of similar red bricks, (see 'A Tudor Eccentricity').

Ellen had the use of each floor of the tower for a specific purpose, hence the much quoted instruction;

> The Lower Room to charity from 7 to 8 o'clock.
> The Second to working tapestry from 9 to 10.
> The Third to music from 10 to noon.
> The Fourth to painting from 12 to 1.
> The Fifth to literature from 1 to 2.
> The Sixth to astronomy at even.

When she had time for lunch we'll never know!

Places of Interest in the Neighbourhood
The Tattingstone Wonder (Tattingstone)
Saint-Maker of Holbrook (Holbrook)
A Tudor Eccentricity (Erwarton)

Freston Tower — room for study.

42 'Old Grog'

Position: Nacton, Suffolk.
OS Map: Ipswich and The Naze area, Sheet 169, 1:50,000.
Map Ref: TM 217 397.
Access: St Martin's Church lies near Orwell Park School, down a lane off the road from Nacton to Levington.

Edward Vernon, local hero and Admiral of the White Squadron of the British Fleet, earned a good reputation by his capture of Portobello for King George II in 1739 when England fought Spain. He also earned the title 'Old Grog' because of the cloak he wore which was made of mixed fibres called grogram. Amongst sailors however, he was not so highly regarded as he was the person responsible for introducing an unpopular practice. In 1740, Admiral Vernon declared that Navy rum rations were henceforth to be watered down, not served neat. Hence the name 'grog' used to describe such concoctions.

Vernon lived in Orwell Park House, now a school, and it is fitting that his monument lies in the church next door. This states; 'In battle, though calm, he was active and though intrepid, prudent, successful yet not ostentatious, ascribing his glory to God.'

Places of Interest in the Neighbourhood
A King's Hiding Place (Ipswich)
England's Last Working Tide Mill (Woodbridge)
A Gothic Folly (Rendlesham)

43 An Elizabethan Conduit

Position: Long Melford, Suffolk.
OS Map: Bury St Edmunds and Sudbury area, Sheet 155. 1:50,000.
Map Ref: TL 865 464.
Access: On the green, where the A1062 meets the A134 Bury – Sudbury road.

Long Melford has the longest village street in England, and is a village packed with historical and architectural interest.

Sitting on the green near the Hall is an Elizabethan conduit built around 1550 to supply water to the Hall and village along wooden pipes. In those days Sir William Cordell owned Melford Hall, and had

Long Melford's Elizabethan conduit.

done so since he took it over in 1547 from the abbey at Bury St Edmunds following its dissolution. Cordell built the Hall (around 1550) and Trinity Hospital (1573). He was a lavish entertainer of royalty and could afford to be so given his influence and power as Solicitor-General and Master of the Rolls.

Of further interest in Long Melford is the 46 metre (153 feet) long Perpendicular church, which has a double-arched monument to Sir William.

Outside a house on the road to Clare there is a remarkable 'crinkle-crankle' wall, probably constructed in this manner to keep heat and sunlight on fruit trees grown in its curves. The entire village is fascinating and well worth exploring to the full.

Places of Interest in the Neighbourhood
Victim of the Poll Tax (Sudbury)
To See Forty Churches (Pentlow)

The Tide Mill at Woodbridge.

44 England's Last Working Tide Mill

Position: Woodbridge, Suffolk.
OS Map: Ipswich and The Naze area, Sheet 169, 1:50,000.
Map Ref: TM 276 487.
Access: On the River Deben, off Quayside and marked on the map as
'Mill' (open to the public).

Sited on the River Deben, the Woodbridge Tide Mill is the only one of
its type remaining in Suffolk, and was the last working tide mill in
England (1957). Its fascinating workings are now fully restored and
operational, contained within a weatherboarded structure of 1793,
though there has been a mill here since Norman times.

  Tide mills are worked by the force of water from a nearby pond which
has been filled by the tide. At high tide the water is locked in the pond
until low tide when it is released to drive the mill wheel. At Woodbridge,
Wyllie's Pond was originally 7½ acres in size and gave two hours working time either side of low tide, which meant four hours of milling each
day. Some mills were capable of double this time. Shipments could be
made easily via the river.

  See the pondwater rush through its channel turning the huge wheel
as it goes – a marvellous feat of engineering, as well as being very
entertaining!

Places of Interest in the Neighbourhood
A Gothic Folly (Rendlesham)
Heroes of the Skies (Parham)
Fortress Against Napoleon (Aldeburgh)
House in the Clouds (Thorpeness)

45 A Gothic Folly

Position: Rendlesham, Suffolk.
OS Map: Saxmundham, Aldeburgh and surrounding area, Sheet 156,
1:50,000.
Map Ref: TM 329 529.
Access: Off the A1152 Melton – Rendlesham road, turn off towards
Rendlesham and Camsey Ash. The folly lies at the end of a short track
on the right.

Short-lived Rendlesham Hall, built in 1871 but burnt down twenty-
seven years later, was demolished in 1949. Still remaining however, are
its older lodges; Ivy Lodge, now a ruin, and Woodbridge Lodge which
is a true Gothic folly. Pevsner, in his marvellous series of *The Buildings
of England*, refers to Woodbridge Lodge as one of the 'most remarkable
follies in Suffolk', and he is quite right.

   The modest Lodge has a central chimney supported by dispropor-
tionate flying buttresses making the entire creation a very comical one.
A good sense of humour was definitely one of this architect's qualities.

Places of Interest in the Neighbourhood
England's Last Working Tide Mill (Woodbridge)
A King's Hiding Place (Ipswich)
'Old Grog' (Nacton)

Woodbridge Lodge, Rendlesham.

46 Heroes of the Skies

Position: Parham, Suffolk.
OS Map: Saxmundham, Aldeburgh and surrounding area, Sheet 156,
1:50,000.
Map Ref: TM 327 607.
Access: Turn off either the A12 opposite Glemham Hall, or the B1116
Hacheston – Framlingham road, through Parham village – follow
signs. (The 390th Bomb Group Memorial Air Museum, entrance free,
open 1-6pm on Sundays and Bank Holidays between April and
October).

Since 1976, dedicated volunteers have carefully restored this Second
World War airfield control tower and packed it with genuine
memorabilia from its past. Such a magnificent job was done in bringing
life to this concrete shell that, in 1991, the 390th Bomb Group
Memorial Air Museum was declared the 'Suffolk Museum of the Year'.

During the war, air bases were dotted all over East Anglia. In 1942,
the government took over land at Parham and constructed the airfield,
which was intended for the Royal Air Force. However, the Americans
took it over in May 1943. From here they flew Flying Fortresses. Many
successful missions were carried out, including raids on Berlin, Kiel and
the Ruhr Valley. On 24th December, 1944, a Flying Fortress called
'Glory Ann II', with full crew and bombs loaded, crashed shortly after
takeoff in the nearby village causing much damage to property and
killing the crew, but without civilian casualties. Photographs of this and
other events are on display.

Also on show are parts of aircraft, uniforms, documents and weapons.
A favourite piece on view is part of Joe Kennedy's Liberator bomber
which exploded over Blythburgh in 1944.

Today, the museum stands as a fitting memorial to all the airmen who
risked their lives during the last war.

Places of Interest in the Neighbourhood
House in the Clouds (Thorpeness)
Fortress Against Napoleon (Aldeburgh)

The 390th Bomb Group Memorial Air Museum.

The Martello Tower at Aldeburgh.

47 Fortress Against Napoleon

Position: Aldeburgh, Suffolk.
OS Map: Saxmundham, Aldeburgh and surrounding area, Sheet 156,
1:50,000.
Map Ref: TM 463 549.
Access: Along the beach road south of Aldeburgh, marked on the map
'Martello Twr' (open to the public).

Sitting squat and sandcastle-like, on a thin peninsula between the North
Sea and the River Alde, is Aldeburgh's Martello Tower. This moulded
fort is just one of 75 hastily erected on the coast between Suffolk and
Sussex against possible invasion by Napoleon in the early 19th century.

Called Martello Towers, after the Torre della Mortella on Corsica
seen by the English army in the 1793-4 War, this one at Aldeburgh was
completed in 1810. It had four guns but was never in action despite
being manned until the middle of Queen Victoria's reign.

These forts were often more problematic than practical, being prone
to damp and usually erected in isolated areas, which made troop
changes awkward. In 1932, the Aldeburgh fort was sold and used as a
private residence until taken over once again by the army in 1940 as a
watch-tower against another enemy in wartime.

Places of Interest in the Neighbourhood
House in the Clouds (Thorpeness)
Heroes of the Skies (Parham)
A Gothic Folly (Rendlesham)

48 House in the Clouds

Position: Thorpeness, Suffolk.
OS Map: Saxmundham, Aldeburgh and surrounding area, Sheet 156, 1:50,000.
Map Ref: TM 468 598.
Access: Off the B1353 at Thorpeness, opposite the windmill.

This remarkable tower is one of the major attractions of a deliberately planned holiday environment of the early 20th century. It is in fact a water tower with living accommodation in the lower part; a splendid disguise to hide what otherwise could have been an eyesore.

Stuart Ogilvie is responsible for the creation of this marvel, set near the sea and facing a man-made lake called The Meare. He planned the village in 1910 and the House in the Clouds was constructed in 1923. Today it is still used for the duel purpose for which it was intended, and, in addition, is a great tourist attraction.

Places of Interest in the Neighbourhood
Fortress Against Napoleon (Aldeburgh)
Heroes of the Skies (Parham)
England's Last Working Tide Mill (Woodbridge)

The disguised water tower at Thorpeness.

49 The Vanished City

Position: Dunwich, Suffolk.
OS Map: Saxmundham, Aldeburgh and surrounding area, Sheet 156, 1:50,000.
Map Ref: TM 476 706 (Museum), TM 477 704 (Friary).
Access: Follow a narrow road to Dunwich from the B1125 Blythburgh – Middleton road, (both locations open to the public).

What caused a large and prosperous city to vanish? This is the question everyone asks when they compare present day Dunwich to the museum model of the city in its heyday. A settlement was already established by the Romans when, in AD630, Sigebert landed here and laid claim to

Monastic remains at Dunwich.

the Kingdom of East Anglia. He appointed Felix as his Bishop in 636 making Dunwich into a city. Four hundred and fifty years later, the Domesday Book records three churches in Dunwich, but by this time the vanishing process had already begun.

At the height of its power and prosperity, in the 12th century, as a city-port, Dunwich possessed many influential citizens and fine buildings. The latter included city walls and gates, a king's palace, nineteen churches, many houses and an outlet to foreign trade long before Yarmouth was established. The sea, once the source of Dunwich's success, now proved to be the harbinger of bad news.

A terrible storm during the reign of Edward III washed away over 400 houses. Sand and shingle blocked up the river port and consequently the city lost the key to its greatness. The citizens refused to give up hope. Elizabeth I (1588-1603) supplied financial support, but, by the end of the 17th century, Dunwich market place was on the beach. Erosion continued to take its toll.

In 1832, electoral reform saw the removal of the right of Dunwich to return a member to parliament. Even in this century sightseers have witnessed churches and houses toppling over the cliffs into the sea. Sacred establishments were swallowed whole forcing the Franciscans to build their friary far inland after their first settlement was washed away in 1288. Parts of the second friary are extant on private land on the cliff top. There is a fine example of a double gateway (through which there is access to the ruins).

Places of Interest in the Neighbourhood
Four Headless Horses (Blythburgh)
St Edmund's Cursed Bridge (Hoxne)
Where the Conqueror's Barons Lived (Bungay)

50 Four Headless Horses

Position: Blythburgh, Suffolk.
OS Map: Saxmundham, Aldeburgh and surrounding area, Sheet 156, 1:50,000.
Map Ref: TM 447 743 (Toby's Walks), TM 454 753 (White Hart Inn).
Access: 'Toby's Walks' is 1·25km/1m SW of Blythburgh on the A12. The White Hart Inn is in the village centre also on the A12.

When the sea mist rolls inland across the Westwood Marshes, blocking out the sunlight, an eerie chill descends upon the heath south of Blythburgh. Suddenly, out of the mask of darkness, an 18th century coach dashes on its way to Yoxford, pulled by four headless horses and driven by a yelling black boy in a drummer-boy's uniform. So relates the tale of Tobias Gill, also known as 'Black Toby'.

Back in 1750, Tobias was serving with Sir Robert Rich's Dragoons in the army of George II. The regiment was encamped at Blythburgh and, having finished his duties for the day, Tobias spent his few pence on beer at the local White Hart Inn. There, he had his last drink.

He was found drunk the following morning on the gravel pit heathland now called 'Toby's Walks'. Next to him lay the dead body of a Walberswick girl, Anne Blakemore. Accused of her murder, Tobias was tried and sentenced to death by hanging in chains.

Black Toby's spirit lives on to taunt us still in this Heritage Coast region of outstanding beauty; stay overnight at your peril!

Places of Interest in the Neighbourhood
The Vanished City (Dunwich)
St Edmund's Cursed Bridge (Hoxne)
Where the Conqueror's Barons Lived (Bungay)

51 St Edmund's Cursed Bridge

Position: Hoxne, Suffolk.
OS Map: Saxmundham, Aldeburgh and surrounding area, Sheet 156,
1:50,000.
Map Ref: TM 179 769 (Goldbrook Bridge), TM 185 767 (Monument).
Access: Goldbrook Bridge is off the B1118 through Hoxne village, take
a left turn after passing over the river. The Hall is right over Goldbrook
Bridge. St Edmund's Monument is marked as such on the map;
continue on the road towards Heckfield and it's in a field on the left.

Bury St Edmunds takes its name from the abbey there which housed the
body of King Edmund. He died at Hoxne in the 9th century and would
have lived longer if it were not for a pair of spurs which he wore on that
day when he was captured by the Danes.

Inguar and his followers were ravaging East Anglia in AD 870, and
took Thetford. Treasure and subservience were demanded of King
Edmund who refused to rule under Inguar's leadership. In the ensuing

The monument marking the place of St Edmund's execution.

battle, Edmund's forces were routed and the king ran off and hid from Inguar under Goldbrook Bridge at Hoxne.

A wedding party, crossing the bridge on its way to the ceremony, noticed Edmund's shiny spurs glinting in the sun as he crouched beneath the bridge. The Danes were alerted, Edmund was captured and subsequently executed by arrows near the place now marked by his monument.

The present Goldbrook Bridge was built in 1878 and has an inscription; 'King Edmund taken prisoner here, AD 870.' On the wall of the nearby Hall we are told that St Edmund was slain near this spot. The monument (supposedly on this spot) replaced an oak tree which collapsed 'by its own weight' in August 1843. Those removing the dead wood are said to have found embedded in it the arrow heads fired into King Edmund.

Legends can cause fear in their effects. Wedding couples are still afraid to pass over Goldbrook Bridge on their special day; Edmund put a curse on the place of his capture, which still holds strong today, over a thousand years after his death.

Places of Interest in the Neighbourhood
Where the Conqueror's Barons Lived (Bungay)
Four Headless Horses (Blythburgh)
The Vanished City (Dunwich)

The ruins of Bungay Castle.

52 Where the Conqueror's Barons Lived

Position: Bungay, Suffolk.
OS Map: Saxmundham, Aldeburgh and surrounding area, Sheet 156, 1:50,000.
Map Ref: TM 335 897.
Access: Bungay Castle lies off The Buttercross on Castle Orchard (open to the public).

Bungay Castle's twin-towered gatehouse has withstood many attempts at its demolition throughout the years. There has been a stronghold here since Norman times when William the Conqueror rewarded Roger Bigod with Bungay for his part in the conquest of England. Here, the Bigod family became entrenched on the border of Norfolk and Suffolk.

Another Bigod, Hugh, built a square castle in 1165 to house the private army with which he ruled this region of East Anglia. So ruthless was he that Henry II decided to put a stop to Bigod's powerful influence over this increasingly prosperous county.

In 1174, Henry ordered the destruction of Bungay Castle after Bigod had ravaged Norwich. The king's engineers planned a vast tunnel to penetrate underneath the castle where a fire would be lit to undermine the foundations. However, Bigod paid a large ransom and the potentially ruinous scheme was halted.

Yet another Roger Bigod rebuilt the castle in 1294; the present gateway is from this period. This version survived into the 15th century when it fell into decay and the stones were used locally for house building.

Many years later Victorian enthusiasts cleared the gatehouse of rubble in an age when ruins influenced art and architecture. It is thanks to this that what we now admire is on view once again.

Places of Interest in the Neighbourhood
Tower of Cubes (Burgh St Peter)
St Edmund's Cursed Bridge (Hoxne)

53 A King's Hiding Place

Position: Buttermarket, Ipswich, Suffolk.
OS Map: Ipswich and The Naze area, Sheet 169. 1:50,000.
Map Ref: TM 164 445.
Access: In the centre of Ipswich, on the corner of Buttermarket and St Stephen's Lane (now a bookshop).

'Pargetting', or decorative plaster work, can be seen in a number of locations in East Anglia. Interesting examples include; Bishop Bonner's Cottage in East Dereham; the Priest's House, Clare, and here in Ipswich where Sparrowe's House of 1670 is a fine specimen (also called Ancient House).

Influenced by Greek and Roman stucco work, Flemish craftsmen introduced pargetting to England in the late 16th century as an elaborate, richly textured decoration to important buildings. It resembles heavy cake icing.

Most spectacular at Sparrowe's House is the painted Royal Arms of Charles II (1630-85). This was probably included in the decoration following Charles' hiding here in a secret room after the Battle of Worcester. Other exciting details can be seen in the high relief symbols from all over the world, presenting an image of internationalism in the days of exploration. The house belonged to a professional trader, William Sparrowe, who must have profited handsomely from his endeavours to afford such a majestic town-house.

Places of Interest in the Neighbourhood
'Old Grog' (Nacton)
England's Last Working Tide Mill (Woodbridge)
A Gothic Folly (Rendlesham)

54 To See Forty Churches

Position: Pentlow, Essex
OS Map: Bury St Edmunds and Sudbury area, Sheet 155, 1:50,000
Map Ref: TL 817 451
Access: At Pentlow, 1·5km/1m south of the A1092 Cavendish – Long
Melford road. Marked on the map as 'Twr' (visible from the road but
lies on private property).

In the old vicarage at Pentlow, and standing 21 metres (70 feet) tall, is
one of England's last true follies. Built as a memorial to the Reverend
J Bull, it was erected in 1859 by his son Edward to a design by
Samual Webb. It is commonly called 'Bull's Tower' or 'Rectory Tower'.
Apparently, if one were to climb the 114 steps to the summit there is a
view of forty churches! I was, however, unable to confirm this.

Places of Interest in the Neighbourhood
An Elizabethan Conduit (Long Melford)
Victim of the Poll Tax (Sudbury)
Soldier of Fortune (Sible Hedingham)

The Ancient House, Ipswich.

55 Dick Turpin's Birthplace

Position: Hempstead, Essex
OS Map: Cambridge and Newmarket, Sheet 154, 1:50,000
Map ref: TL 633 380
Access: On the B1054 Hempstead – Steeple Bumpstead road.

Epping Forest's dense woodland is still much in evidence today. Its lanes are thickly shrouded by trees, as they were in the 18th century when highwayman Dick Turpin (1705-1739) used this area as a hideout. Legend portrays Turpin rather romantically when, in fact, he was a vicious vagabond who preyed on innocent citizens in and around Epping. Highway robbery was common here and concealed within is the secret 'Dick Turpin's Cave', one of his many retreats.

Turpin was born here in the Bell Inn, Hempstead. Opposite the house is a bridge and a small pond where Turpin must have watered his steed.

Having trained as a butcher in Whitechapel, Turpin turned to cattle and deer stealing, smuggling and robbery. He formed a ruthless gang without mercy in its quest for riches. Turpin once held a local woman over her own fire in order to force her into revealing the whereabouts of her savings.

A huge campaign was waged against Turpin and special militia were raised to track him down in the surrounding forests. When the net was closing in Turpin escaped and fled to Yorkshire, changing his name to John Palmer. There, Turpin continued a life of crime. He even accidentally killed his partner Tom King in one daring exit from a hold-up. But his adventures ended with his capture while horse stealing. On 7th April, 1739 he was hanged in York. And so ended the short career of one of Essex's most feared sons.

Places of Interest in the Neighbourhood
Locks and Stocks (Great Bardfield)
Soldiers of Fortune (Sible Hedingham)
A Victorian 'Cholera Pump' (Earls Colne)

Where Dick Turpin was born.

56 Soldier of Fortune

Position: Sible Hedingham, Essex
OS Map: Bury St Edmunds and Sudbury area, Sheet 155, 1:50,000
Map Ref: TL 776 344
Access: Sible Hedingham church is off the A604, on the road to High Street Green (open Sundays).

Churches are rich in curiosities of many kinds, as is evident throughout this book. Here in St Peter's church lies the tomb of Sir John Hawkwood (1340-1394), who was a mighty and ruthless medieval knight. He became enthralled by power politics abroad during the Hundred Years War.

Hawkwood, son of a tanner, was born in Sible Hedingham and was knighted by Edward III. His quest for adventure took him abroad with the king and the Black Prince and he saw victory at Poitiers and Crecy in 1356. Hawkwood then became a mercenary knight, fighting for those who would pay the most. He made his fortune in Italy, which at that time was a collection of principalities, all warring with each other.

In Italy, Hawkwood founded the 'White Company' of knights in 1359 and sold his services to the lords of the 'City States'. In 1364, he assisted Agnello in becoming Doge of Pisa. Five years later he was captured by the Pope's army and ransomed. A true Machiavellian, Hawkwood made his name as a fierce fighter, was promoted to General of the Florentine army in 1390, and married the daughter of the Duke of Milan. When he died he was buried in the Duomo cathedral of Florence. In commemoration, there is a magnificent fresco by Paolo Uccello showing Hawkwood on horseback painted in 1436. It is believed that the body was returned to Essex and lies buried beneath the Hawkwood memorial in the south aisle of St Peter's church.

Places of Interest in the Neighbourhood
A Victorian 'Cholera Pump' (Earls Colne)
Locks and Stocks (Great Bardfield)
Dick Turpin's Birthplace (Hempstead)

57 Robert Adam's Towers

Position: Mistley, Essex
OS Map: Ipswich and The Naze area, Sheet 169, 1:50,000
Map Ref: TM 116 320
Access: At the junction of the Manningtree – Harwich and Mistley – Colchester (B1352) roads, marked on the map as 'Towers'.

Just on the south bank of Seafield Bay, where the River Stour widens at Mistley, there stands a pair of odd-looking towers which appear lost and are abandoned. These are all that remain of Robert Adam's 18th century church, begun in 1776. It had been built for Richard Rigby, Paymaster General 1768-1784, as an impressive addition to his vast estate. Rigby was an extravagant party-giver and it is said that he employed servants in shifts to keep the entertainments going day and night.

In 1870 the nave of the church was pulled down, leaving the neo-classical twin-towers as rare evidence of Robert Adam's church ar-

Mistley Towers.

chitecture. This Scottish architect (1728-1792) was a key figure in Britain's neo-classical revolution and had been greatly influenced by the ancients while on the 'Grand Tour' of Italy. With his brother James, he published *Works in Architecture*; a detailed reference work in furnishing design. Other Adam delights include; Syon House and Osterley Park (Middlesex), Gunton Church (Norfolk), Theatre and Market Hall (Bury St Edmunds), and Audley End interiors (Essex).

Places of Interest in the Neighbourhood
Unjustly Executed (Dovercourt)
The Kaiser's Gift (Dovercourt)
A Warning to Sailors (Walton-on-the-Naze)

The memorial to Captain Fryatt, Dovercourt.

58 Unjustly Executed

Position: Dovercourt, Essex
OS Map: Ipswich and The Naze area, Sheet 169, 1:50,000
Map Ref: TM 238 311
Access: The Fryatt memorial is at the far end of All Saint's churchyard, on Main Road.

Buried at Dovercourt is the body of Captain Charles Algernon Fryatt, shot by the enemy in the First World War. He is a great British hero.

The story began in 1915 when Captain Fryatt's Great Eastern Railway steamship *Brussels* rammed the German submarine U-boat 33, which had been chasing his ship. Non-military ships had been attacked previously and Fryatt did what he could to see off this potential threat. On his return to port the Admiralty praised Fryatt and awarded him a gold watch.

The following year, while crossing the Channel from Tilbury to Holland, Captain Fryatt's ship was intercepted and he was taken prisoner. His act of 28th March, 1915 was declared unlawful, despite his being in uniform at the time. Fryatt was executed on 27th July, 1916.

The British government, press and people immediately condemned the shooting and defended Captain Fryatt's action in protecting his ship and crew against the U-boat, especially when it was German policy to sink merchant ships. Up to August 1916, forty unarmed vessels had been sunk by the German navy.

After the war, Captain Fryatt's body was returned to Dovercourt and buried here with full military honours.

Places of Interest in the Neighbourhood
The Kaiser's Gift (Dovercourt)
A Warning to Sailors (Walton-on-the-Naze)
Robert Adam's Towers (Mistley)

59 Locks and Stocks

Position: (1) Great Bardfield, (2) Bradwell-on-Sea, (3) Canewdon,
Essex
OS Map: (1) Chelmsford, Harlow and surrounding area, Sheet 167,
1:50,000, (2&3) Colchester and The Blackwater area, Sheet 168,
1:50,000
Map Refs: TL 676 307 (Great Bardfield); TM 005 069
(Bradwell-on-Sea); TQ 897 945 (Canewdon)
Access: (1) Just south of the long bridge on the B1057 Great Bardfield –
Finchingfield road (open to the public 2-6, Sat, Sun, Bank Hol Mon,
Easter – Sept). (2) Next to the church and opposite the school on the
Roman Road to St Peter's Chapel (see Chapel on a Roman Wall). (3)
Behind the church, at entrance to churchyard.

In medieval England many Essex villages would have had their own jail
for local wrong-doers. Three such buildings, though not medieval, have
survived in good order. Great Bardfield cage can be explored in detail.
That at Bradwell (1817) has some old restraining irons attached where
prisoners cooled their heels.

The lock-up at Bradwell-on-Sea.

Great Bardfield Cage.

Canewdon lock-up is from the 18th century and lies next to the church, but has not always been so near. It was moved to its present site in 1938; perhaps as a deliberate reminder to parishioners to keep to the straight and narrow! Visible within are the old village stocks. A notice pinned to the jail refers to the 1351 'Statute of Labourers' which required every town to use stocks as a form of punishment.

This law followed the 1347 outbreak of the Black Death in the reign of Edward III. It was an attempt to return prices and wages to the levels found before the plague. Half the population perished in that outbreak, making labour scarce. Those who could work demanded high wages to keep up with rising prices of increasingly scarce foodstuffs. The Statute tried to deal with this situation by declaring that all labourers under 60 years of age were to be paid wages at the levels of 1340. The main effect of the law was to prevent workers from having a say in their conditions of employment. Special Justices were appointed to administer the penalties to offenders; hence, jails were built to house these unfortunates.

Places of Interest in the Neighbourhood
Great Bardfield:
Soldier of Fortune (Sible Hedingham)
A Victorian 'Cholera Pump' (Earls Colne)
Bradwell-on-Sea:
Chapel on a Roman Wall (Bradwell-on-Sea)
Canewdon:
Leviathans Over Essex (Great Burstead)
A Victorian Spiderman (Stock)

60 A Victorian 'Cholera Pump'

Position: Earls Colne, Essex
OS Map: Colchester and The Blackwater area, Sheet 168, 1:50.000
Map Ref: TL 863 285
Access: At Pound Green, on the Coggeshall Road (where the B1024 joins the A604).

Some Victorians liked to do charitable works, especially if they had wealth. One such benefactor was Mary Gee, born in 1795. She left behind an impressive string of endowments and gifts, of which this intriguing 'Cholera Pump' is just one.

Mary Gee had it erected in 1853, 'In thankful commemoration for the absence of cholera', and to supply fresh water to the citizens of East Colne; though it is uncertain if it ever produced drinkable water.

Other legacies include a charity school in Maplestead (1836, rebuilt 1863), Earls Colne School (1836), and assistance with the building of two churches; Halstead (1843), and Greenstead Green (1845). She died in 1864.

Places of Interest in the Neighbourhood
Soldier of Fortune (Sible Hedingham)
Locks and Stocks (Great Bardfield)
Dick Turpin's Birthplace (Hempstead)

The 'Cholera Pump' at Earls Colne.

61 A Warning to Sailors

Position: Walton-on-the-Naze, Essex
OS Map: Ipswich and The Naze area, Sheet 169, 1:50,000
Map Ref: TM 265 235
Access: From Walton-on-the-Naze follow signs to 'The Naze', marked
on the map as 'Tower', car park at entrance.

Coastal lighthouses are run by the Trinity House Corporation with
revenue collected from ships visiting English ports. This organisation
descends from a medieval association of 'Pilots' whose job it was to

The Naze Tower at Walton.

operate lighthouses up until 1894 when these were brought under public control.

Sailors have looked towards The Naze tower for guidance ever since it was raised by Trinity House in 1719 (though it is a tower rather than a lighthouse). Being on top of The Naze cliffs and reaching a height of 24 metres (81 feet), it is visible for many miles out at sea. There are sandbanks just off shore making the need for vigilance a priority for shipping approaching Harwich and Felixstowe just north of The Naze point.

This octagonal, embattled landmark is situated in a pleasant picnic site and nature reserve.

Places of Interest in the Neighbourhood
Unjustly Executed (Dovercourt)
The Kaiser's Gift (Dovercourt)
Robert Adam's Towers (Mistley)

The Flitch chair, St Mary's church, Little Dunmow.

62 Bacon for the Bride

Position: Little Dunmow, Essex
OS Map: Chelmsford, Harlow and surrounding area, Sheet 167,
1:50,000
Map Ref: TL 656 212
Access: St Mary's church is just south of the village. Collect the key at
the 'Flitch of Bacon' pub, turn down Brook Street and St Mary's Place.

In the bar of the 'Flitch of Bacon' pub at Little Dunmow, there is a 'pig
clock' and other objects connected with bacon. Curiosity is immediately
aroused. Soon, one discovers that the village is very famous for its
ancient custom of the 'Dunmow Flitch'. A quaint verse on the pub wall
adds further intrigue:

> Painted in gold ye flitch behold,
> Of famed Dunmow ye boaste,
> Then here should call fond couples all,
> And pledge it in a toaste.

The custom of the flitch centred around married couples who had
stayed loyal for one year and a day. Together they gathered at Little
Dunmow and were interrogated. The winning pair were awarded a side
or 'flitch' of bacon and carried ceremoniously at shoulder height in the
flitch chair, which can be seen in St Mary's church.

The custom probably originated at the church – then a priory, in an
effort to encourage good relationships in marriage. Richard Wright of
Bawburgh, Norwich was the first recorded winner in 1445. Since then,
the tradition has been followed intermittently. The last genuine award
in 1751 was made to Thomas and Anne Shakeshaft of Wethersfield,
who sold off bits of the bacon for profit!

In the 19th century, William Harrison Ainsworth restarted the
ceremony with a jury deciding the winner. These events, held at Great
Dunmow, were often rowdy and attracted vast numbers.

As with all traditional customs, songs and verses emerged to celebrate
this unique event. It was mentioned in the 14th century poem *Piers the
Plowman*: 'Thei don hem to Donemowe, To folwen for the flicche'.
And Chaucer refers to 'The Bacon' in the *Wife of Bath* tale: 'That some
men have in Essex at Dunmowe'.

Stay awhile here in the church, the former Lady Chapel of the priory,
and see some of the many other historical objects on show; the tomb of
Matilda, daughter of Robert Fitzwalter who led the Barons against

King John with the Magna Carta; and, in the aisle, the floor slab of John Wylde aged 9 months who was brought to Essex to escape the London plague of 1665, but died shortly after his arrival here. The flitch chair is 13th century, probably the end of a row of chairs which was adapted for the flitch ceremony in the 15th century.

Places of Interest in the Neighbourhood
Felsted's Hooved Woman (Felsted)
Most Evil Essex Man (Felsted)

A doll's house, Hollytrees Museum.

63 House of Curios

Position: Colchester, Essex
OS Map: Colchester and The Blackwater area, Sheet 168, 1:50,000
Map Ref: TM 000 253
Access: Hollytrees museum is on High Street, next to the castle (open to the public, Mon – Sat 10am – 1pm/2pm – 5pm, entrance free). Gray's Folly is in the castle grounds.

Solicitor Charles Gray (1696-1782) brought wealth into his family in 1726 when he married Sarah Creffield. They lived next to Colchester castle in 'Hollytrees', now a museum. Gray had a passionate interest in the history of Colchester and was keen to restore the castle from a heap of battered rubble into a model of its former glory. As a member of the Castle Museum Committee, he put much of his wealth and time into its restoration just ninety years after the Civil War had virtually destroyed it. Following that event, much of the castle stone was sold as building material.

Gray continued his hard work, even after becoming the member of parliament for Colchester, and improved the north-east tower in 1746, and much of the interior of the main part of the castle. He sympathetically cleared the grounds, adding his folly arch which was built over an old dovecote.

Gray's Georgian town house (1718) is now an Aladdin's cave of curios; toys, dolls, games, prams, furniture and paintings, including a 1911 view of Colchester by Pissarro, and a portrait of Gray in the entrance hall. Upstairs there are scientific instruments, uniforms and costumes. Both house and arch serve as a memorial to Gray and his magnificent efforts in restoring Colchester Castle. He is buried in All Saint's church.

Places of Interest in the Neighbourhood (all in Colchester)
Evidence of a Siege
A Tower Called 'Jumbo'
The Pub in the Wall
Merry Old Soul
Obelisk to Bloodshed
Minories Folly

64 Evidence of a Siege

Position: Colchester, Essex
OS Map: Colchester and The Blackwater area, Sheet 168, 1:50,000
Map Ref: TM 007 253
Access: Leave the town via East Hill; Siege House lies just beyond the bridge on East Street.

Specially highlighted holes in the exterior of a 16th century house in Colchester have a rather peculiar origin. During the latter half of the English Civil War of 1648, Colchester took the side of the Parliamentarians against the Royalists and Charles I. Parliament had just tried to limit the king's power, especially over taxation, and in readiness to repel the Royalists Colchester's soldiers took over this timber-framed house next to the bridge at the entrance to the city. It was rapidly converted into a guardhouse.

A siege ensued once the Royalists attacked, and the timbers of this 'Siege House' became peppered with lead shot. These wounds have been carefully marked by red metal rings on the outside of the building which can be clearly seen.

Places of Interest in the Neighbourhood (all in Colchester)
House of Curios
A Tower Called 'Jumbo'
The Pub in the Wall
Merry Old Soul
Obelisk to Bloodshed
Minories Folly

The Siege House, Colchester.

65 A Tower called 'Jumbo'

Position: Colchester, Essex
OS Map: Colchester and The Blackwater area, Sheet 168, 1:50,000
Map Ref: TL 993 252
Access: Jumbo water tower lies behind Head Street, near the Balkerne Gate.

In the 1880's, American circus owner Phineas Taylor Barnum (1810-1891), along with James Bailey, promoted 'The Greatest Show on Earth'. It was an exciting extravaganza, carefully compiled to delight late-Victorian society and to make lots of money. As experienced purveyors of the freakish and unusual, Barnum and Bailey became very successful, and never more so than with their 6½ ton African elephant called 'Jumbo'.

Ever since the 1880's the name 'Jumbo' has been used to describe anything enormous. Colchester water tower justly deserves this name as it is over 30 metres (100 feet) high, and holds 230,000 gallons of water. This brick monster, with its four giant arches and central access column, is a wonderful example of late-Victorian majestic enterprise. It can be seen from many places across the city.

Places of Interest in the Neighbourhood (all in Colchester)
House of Curios
Evidence of a Siege
The Pub in the Wall
Merry Old Soul
Obelisk to Bloodshed
Minories Folly

'Jumbo' water tower, Colchester.

66 The Pub in the Wall

Position: Colchester, Essex
OS Map: Colchester and The Blackwater area, Sheet 168,1:50,000
Map Ref: TL 992 252
Access: The Hole in the Wall pub is just next to the Balkerne Gate ruins on Balkerne Hill.

At the west end of Roman Camulodunum (Colchester), the oldest town in Britain, stood the Balkerne Gate which served as the main entrance into the town. Its ruined hulk, built around AD200, remains today and is one of the largest Roman gateways in existence.

Leading off the Balkerne Gate is a short stretch of wall. Neatly tucked into this is a delightful pub which just fits a convenient gap in the town's defences, hence its name; 'Hole in the Wall'. It is built directly above an ancient Roman guardhouse and carriageway.

Places of Interest in the Neighbourhood (all in Colchester)
House of Curios
Evidence of a Siege
A Tower Called 'Jumbo'
Merry Old Soul
Obelisk to Bloodshed
Minories Folly

The Hole in the Wall pub, Colchester.

67 Merry Old Soul

Position: Colchester, Essex
OS Map: Colchester and The Blackwater area, Sheet 168, 1:50,000
Map Ref: TL 996 252
Access: The Town Hall is on High Street.

Interesting architectural features often go unnoticed, especially in busy shopping centres. One such item stands at the summit of the late- Victorian Town Hall in Colchester; the figure of St Helena. Who was she and why put her here?

Helena (AD 242-330) was the daughter of King Coel of East Anglia who ruled from Camulodunum (as Colchester was then called). He built the city around AD 219, and the name Colchester is thought to have

The Statue of St Helena, Colchester Town Hall.

evolved from 'Coel' and 'Chester' – the Roman for city. He was also the subject of the famous nursery rhyme;

> Old King Cole was a merry old soul,
> And a merry old soul was he.

Helena was his only child and destined for leadership in a Europe led by Romans. King Coel headed a rebellion against Roman occupation but was thwarted in his ambitions when Helena fell in love with Constantius Chlorus, head of the Roman army, and peace was made so that they could marry.

She was converted to Christianity, and gave birth to Rome's first Christian emperor, Constantine the Great. By the Edict of Milan in AD313, Rome adopted Christianity. Hence, a daughter of Essex changed the course of religious development and history itself. She went on to become a saint following her reputed discovery of the True Cross. Little wonder King Coel was so merry.

Places of Interest in the Neighbourhood (all in Colchester)
House of Curios
Evidence of a Siege
A Tower Called 'Jumbo'
The Pub in the Wall
Obelisk to Bloodshed
Minories Folly

The Lucas & Lisle Memorial.

68 Obelisk to Bloodshed

Position: Colchester, Essex
OS Map: Colchester and The Blackwater area, Sheet 168, 1:50,000
Map Ref: TL 999 254
Access: In the castle grounds on the north side (High Street).

The citizens of 17th century Colchester were prepared to compromise in time of war to save their ancient city. However, in June 1648, this tactic had disastrous consequences for the city.

At the end of the English Civil War Parliamentarian Colchester was persuaded by its leaders to allow the opposing Royalist army inside the city walls rather than risk a fight. This displeased the national Parliamentarian 'New Model Army', and Colchester was attacked by them under Thomas Lord Fairfax.

Meanwhile, Colchester's new Royalist masters forced the citizens to defend the city against their former ally. It was a long, hot summer. Food was scarce and disease took a mighty toll. Fairfax used the shortage of food to starve Colchester into submission. Once all the animals had been eaten, the city surrendered on 27th August.

No mercy was given to the Royalist leaders. Three were executed; Sir Charles Lucas, Sir George Lisle and Sir Arthur Lord Capel – he was executed at the Tower of London. Lucas and Lisle were shot behind Colchester Castle. In a very brash manner, Lisle dared the firing squad to come near in case they missed their target. One of the soldiers replied, 'I'll warrant ye Sir, we'll hit you!' Lisle retorted, 'Friend, I have been nearer when you have missed me.'

At the spot of their execution stands this obelisk marking one of the bloodiest events in East Anglian history. It gives the date of execution as 28th August, 1648. Both men were buried in St Giles' church.

Places of Interest in the Neighbourhood (all in Colchester)
House of Curios
Evidence of a Siege
A Tower Called 'Jumbo'
The Pub in the Wall
Merry Old Soul
Minories Folly

69 Minories Folly

Position: Colchester, Essex
OS Map: Colchester and The Blackwater area, Sheet 168, 1:50,000
Map Ref: TM 000 252
Access: On East Hill, opposite Hollytrees Museum, (entrance free).

In the grounds of the Minories there is a Gothic Summer House, once called the Dovecote. It is a mixture of arches, embattlements and niches in brick and looks very medieval. It appears on an 18th century map as being at the end of a long drive from St James' church. Now it makes an elegant backdrop to the Minories Art Gallery and cafeteria.

Alderman Thomas Boggis upgraded and improved the house in 1776. It had been in his family since 1731 when it was bought by Issac Boggis, a wealthy baymaker in the woollen trade. Since the 18th century, the Minories has been used by medical professionals and as this splendid art gallery since 1958.

Places of Interest in the Neighbourhood (all in Colchester)
House of Curios
Evidence of a Siege
A Tower Called 'Jumbo'
The Pub in the Wall
Merry Old Soul
Obelisk to Bloodshed

The Minories Folly, Colchester.

70 The Kaiser's Gift

Position: Dovercourt, Essex
OS Map: Ipswich and The Naze area, Sheet 169, 1:50,000
Map Ref: TM 238 311
Access: All Saint's church is on Main Road, (see also Unjustly
Executed).

It seems a mystery why the German Kaiser should supply a church in
Dovercourt with a stained glass window! It shows Our Lord and a
Centurion; the seemingly unlikely union of religion and war. Here it is
displayed, in the side of the tower, as a memorial to the dead of the
ill-fated Walcheren expedition of 1809.

In the reign of George III, England and Germany were both at
war with revolutionary France which was under the dictatorship of
Napoleon. As part of the long war against change in Europe, a major
expedition was sent to Walcheren Island at the mouth of the River
Scheldt, in Holland. Its purpose was to secure the area and prevent the
French navy from operating from Antwerp. Lord Chatham led the
expedition and it embarked from Portsmouth and Deal in July 1809.
This was the greatest fleet ever to have left England; 40,000 troops, 35
ships and 200 other support vessels.

On arrival in Holland, the troops dug in and awaited orders. Heat and
floods caused by broken dykes led to an outbreak of malaria and
typhoid. Without any engagement of the enemy 11,000 troops were
shipped home with fever, of which 4,000 died. The mission was a
complete failure. The sick were badly treated; housed in damp and
overcrowded buildings without adequate food, clothing or medicine.
English medical support for troops continued to be insufficient until the
efforts of Florence Nightingale, in similar circumstances during the
Crimean War of 1854, opened the way to better provision.

Places of Interest in the Neighbourhood
Unjustly Executed (Dovercourt)
A Warning to Sailors (Walton-on-the-Naze)
Robert Adam's Towers (Mistley)

71 Felsted's Hooved Woman

Position: Felsted, Essex
OS Map: Chelmsford, Harlow and surrounding area, Sheet 167,
1:50,000
Map Ref: TL 677 203
Access: On the corner of Braintree Road and Chelmsford Road; 'The
Boote House'.

George Boote had a sense of humour, or a dislike of a particular
woman. On the corner of a house he built in the 16th century is a
painted carving of the 'Old Hag of Felsted'. She is gazing down, with a
stern and sour look, on all who dare to pass beneath her hooved feet.
Could she have been Boote's wife?

The inscription on the side of the house reads; 'George Boote made
this house, 1596'. Thankfully, this building has been well maintained
and now is used as a restaurant.

Places of Interest in the Neighbourhood
Most Evil Essex Man (Felsted)
Bacon for the Bride (Little Dunmow)
Locks and Stocks (Great Bardfield)

72 Most Evil Essex Man

Position: Felsted, Essex
OS Map: Chelmsford, Harlow and surrounding area, Sheet 167,
1:50,000
Map Ref: TL 677 204
Access: Holy Cross church is on Braintree Road.

Holy Cross church has a huge memorial to Richard Rich, 1st Baron of
Leighs (1496-1567) which, in itself, is not unusual. The presence of the
memorial today seems incomprehensible as Richard Rich was probably
the most evil Essex man.

Lord Rich had more power over the destinies of men than many
kings did. Serving under Henry VIII (1491-1547), he became Solicitor
General in 1533, Speaker of the Commons in 1536, Privy Councillor in
1540 and Lord Chancellor in 1547 to the new King Edward VI (1537-
1553). Under Henry VIII, Lord Rich assisted in the 'Dissolution of the
Monasteries' and transferred much church property to the Crown and
to himself. He took possession of Leighs Priory and built a house there,

The Rich Memorial, Holy Cross church.

as well as acquiring over 100 manors in Essex. He was single-minded, ruthless and an opportunist who switched sides to suit himself.

His most evil actions earned Lord Rich the post of Chancellor of the Court of Augmentations from 1536-1544. He prosecuted the Bishop of Rochester and Sir Thomas More when Henry VIII took over as head of the church in England. Rochester defended the supremacy of the Pope against the King, was imprisoned and found guilty of high treason. He was beheaded at Tyburn. Sir Thomas More opposed the Act of Supremacy of 1534, and he too was beheaded.   Further evidence of Lord Rich's opportunism occurred when Edward VI declared Lady Jane Grey his successor and was supported by Lord Rich. She was actually proclaimed Queen in 1553, but beheaded nine days later. Lord Rich quickly voiced his support for Mary Tudor (later Mary I), and during her reign he went on to persecute Protestants in Essex, adding to the Queen's reputation as 'Bloody Mary'.

Places of Interest in the Neighbourhood
Felsted's Hooved Woman (Felsted)
Bacon for the Bride (Little Dunmow)
Locks and Stocks (Great Bardfield)

73 Tallest Gatehouse

Position: Layer Marney, Essex
OS Map: Colchester and The Blackwater area, Sheet 168, 1:50,000
Map Ref: TL 928 175
Access: Turn off the B1022 Tiptree – Colchester road, following signs to 'Layer Marney Tower' (open to the public).

Firmly entrenched in this quiet part of Essex is the tallest Tudor gatehouse in Britain; Layer Marney Tower. It is a magnificent terracotta and brick built structure of eight storeys in four towers. It was built

Layer Marney Tower gatehouse.

purely for show in the grand Tudor style of 1520, and reminds one very much of Oxburgh Hall gatehouse in Norfolk (1482).

The Marney family had been here since the 12th century and reached its peak under Sir Henry Marney, Privy Councillor to Henry VIII. He had great plans for a huge hall here, but he died in 1523 leaving the house unbuilt. The tower, and the smaller east and west wings attached, are all that exist of his ambitious schemes. Designed by Italian Girolamo de Travizi, the tower is 24 metres (80 feet) high and embodies Marney's passion for the Italianate taste which he admired so much while abroad. This prestigious and boastful fashion soon faded and Layer Marney remains the last built evidence of the defensive style in stately architecture.

See the tombs of the Marney family in the nearby church, dating from 1414.

Places of Interest in the Neighbourhood
Leviathans Over Essex (Great Wigborough)
Locks and Stocks (Bradwell-on-Sea)
Chapel on a Roman Wall (Bradwell-on-Sea)

74 Leviathans Over Essex

Position: (1) Great and Little Wigborough, (2) Great Burstead, Essex
OS Maps: (1) Colchester and The Blackwater area, Sheet 168, 1:50,000
         (2) East London area, Sheet 177, 1:50,000
Map Refs: (1) Great Wigborough TL 968 157
           Little Wigborough TL 981 145
         (2) Great Burstead TQ 681 923
Access: Great Wigborough; St Stephen's church is signposted 'church'
off the Tolleshunt D'Arcy – Peldon road.
Little Wigborough; St Nicholas' church is at Copt Hall, south of the
village.
Great Burstead; St Mary's church is just off the A176 Billericay –
Basildon road.

The first real air weapons of terror and destruction were tried and tested
over the towns and villages of East Anglia during the First World
War. On the night of 23rd September, 1916, two German airships or
'Zeppelins', entered British air space with intent to kill. Both flying
monsters failed to return to base.

At Great Wigborough, just north of the River Blackwater, Zeppelin
L33 met its end. Having been hit by gunfire over Bromley (where it
had killed six civilians by bombing), L33 finally crashed here. There is
a contemporary record of this event in St Stephen's church, framed
by aluminium from the wrecked Zeppelin. Captain Aloys Bocker and
his crew of twenty reluctantly ditched their airship, set it on fire, and
walked towards nearby Peldon. On the way they were apprehended by
special constable Edgar Nichols who took them single-handedly into
custody.

At St Nicholas' church, Little Wigborough, a portion of the crashed
airship can be seen hanging over the tower arch. This church is very
close to the actual spot where L33 landed.

A sister ship, L32, was also shot down and all 22 crew were killed
at Great Burstead. This monster had flown from Nordholz in northern Germany, and was captained by Werner Peterson, a navy man.
Frederick Sowery shot down the L32 shortly after he had taken off from
Hornchurch. All the crew were buried in a corner of the churchyard of
St Mary Magdalen at Great Burstead and then returned to Germany
during the Nazi era. All that now remain are a few stones from the
original graveside.

Of further interest inside St Mary's is the 900 year old chest used to collect money for the Crusades, and some medieval wall paintings.

Places of Interest in the Neighbourhood
Great and Little Wigborough:
Tallest Gatehouse (Layer Marney)
Locks and Stocks (Bradwell-on-Sea)
Chapel on a Roman Wall (Bradwell-on-Sea)
Great Burstead:
A Victorian Spiderman (Stock)
Locks and Stocks (Canewdon)

St Cedd's chapel, AD654.

75 Chapel on a Roman Wall

Position: Bradwell-on-Sea, Essex
OS Map: Colchester and The Blackwater area, Sheet 168, 1:50,000
Map Ref: TM 031 082
Access: At Bradwell, take the Roman Road from the church.

When the Romans left Essex to contend with problems closer to Rome, they left behind, at Bradwell-on-Sea, a fort called Othona. A few hundred years later, St Cedd arrived at this marshy place where he intended to convert the local Saxons to Christianity.

In AD654, Cedd was appointed Bishop and his first step was to erect a chapel over the ruined wall of the Roman fort. Here it still reigns as one of the first English churches. St Cedd's or St Peter's on the Wall, is best admired in its setting; isolated and windswept yet dominant on this flat horizon; the atmosphere is almost mystical.

St Cedd's conquest of paganism was shortlived however. He died of yellow fever in 664 at Lastingham, in Yorkshire. The East Anglian Saxons were convinced that this event was caused by the anger of their old gods at having been abandoned, so they returned to their pagan culture.

Places of Interest in the Neighbourhood
Locks and Stocks (Bradwell-on-Sea)
A Victorian Spiderman (Stock)
Leviathans Over Essex (Great Burstead)

76 Oldest Wooden Church

Position: Greensted, Essex
OS Map: Chelmsford, Harlow and surrounding area, Sheet 167,
1:50,000
Map Ref: TL 539 030
Access: 1·5km/1m southwest of Chipping Ongar, marked on the map as
'Log Church'.

Dedicated to St Andrew, this remarkable church lays claim to being the
oldest wooden one in existence. It is Saxon in origin and its builders
used wood from the surrounding forest of Epping, which was in
plentiful supply. The present logs are those same ones cut by the Saxons
in AD845 when the nave was built upon the site of an earlier chapel,
probably of the 7th or 8th century. These walls are of whole split
upright logs and would have originally supported a crude thatched
roof.

A look around the wooden nave exterior reveals many curiosities.
There is a filled space of the earliest doorway, an eye-hole and a niche.
The brick base is of much later construction, as is the Tudor chancel
and roof.

Greensted Church was once used as a temporary resting place for the
body of St Edmund who had been martyred in the 9th century by the
Danes (see St Edmund's Cursed Bridge). The dead king's body had
been kept at Bury St Edmunds and then moved to London away from
possible vandalism by marauding invaders. By 1013, it was considered
safe enough to return the body to Bury and, on the journey northwards,
St Andrew's at Greensted was used as a suitable stopping place (inside
the church there is a splendid St Edmund window). Later additions
to the fabric, especially the tower, are tastefully done and the whole
impression is one of harmony.

Places of Interest in the Neighbourhood
Memorial to a Horse (Loughton)
King Harold's Resting Place (Waltham Abbey)
A Fantasy Grotto (Wanstead)

The Saxon church, Greensted.

77 King Harold's Resting Place

Position: Waltham Abbey, Essex
OS Map: Luton and Hertford, Sheet 166, 1:50,000
Map Ref: TL 383 007
Access: Off the A112 at Waltham Abbey. Follow signs to Abbey car park. Harold's stone is in front of the east end of the church.

Most school children know that King Harold was killed at Hastings in 1066 by an arrow in the eye. But, do they know he was buried at Waltham Abbey in Essex?

By the age of 23, Harold II (1022-1066) was Earl of East Anglia. In 1058, he visited Rome and was inspired enough to build his own church here at Waltham. He rested at his mansion on his way south to fight the invader William of Normandy in 1066. Having won a battle in the north of England, Harold hastily assembled an army to repel the French. The battle which followed changed the course of history. Harold died on the 14th October, and was conveyed to his abbey at Waltham by the monks Osgod and Ailric. There he was buried at the high altar. This site was destroyed at the Dissolution, and now there is a stone marking the spot where the body lies.

Typically, there is a conflicting story that Harold was interred further back from the church in an orchard. Its owner once dug up the coffin to sell the lead! However, we cannot be sure this ever happened.

Also in the area; visit the excavated foundations of a 13th century forge near the car park, and the Epping Forest District Museum on Sun Street – this contains historical items within a 400 year old house (entrance free), many of which are connected to the abbey, including an abbot's skeleton!

Places of Interest in the Neighbourhood
Memorial to a Horse (Loughton)
A Fantasy Grotto (Wanstead)

The tomb of King Harold.

78 A Victorian Spiderman

Position: Stock, Essex
OS Map: Chelmsford, Harlow and surrounding area, Sheet 167,
1:50,000
Map Ref: TQ 691 989
Access: Just off the B1007 Billericay – Chelmsford road at Stock.

Nestled comfortably in the pleasant village of Stock is this 15th century pub, The Bear Inn, which has an engaging tale to tell.

During the Victorian era, the inn had an ostler named Charlie Marshall who knew the pub well, especially its fireplaces and their interlinking chimneys. He lived in the inn stables and was an untidy soul, once described as 'lousy as hedge-pig'.

Charlie had a favourite trick; for a bet or a pint, he would disappear up a chimney in one bar and reappear in the fireplace of another! Often he would stay up the labyrinth and sleep off his drink. In this case, the locals would burn straw or paper to flush him out. One day he vanished completely.

The tale is still told that Charlie died up the chimney, embarrassing the inn keeper by his death. To clear their consciences, the locals built a coffin, filled it with bricks, and prepared to have it buried only to be rejected by the church. It was dumped in a rough grave nearby. It is also rumoured that a body was found up the chimney during some buildings alterations many years later!

Places of Interest in the Neighbourhood
Leviathans Over Essex (Great Burstead)
Locks and Stocks (Canewdon)

79 Memorial to a Horse

Position: Loughton, Essex
OS Map: Chelmsford, Harlow and surrounding area, Sheet 167,
1:50,000
Map Ref: TQ 410 958
Access: The monument lies in a field called 'The Warren' and is marked
on the map as 'Mon'. It is just off the A104 running through Epping
Forest. There is a parking place on the right between The Warren and
the Robin Hood roundabout just north of it. Walk along the main road
until the monument comes into view (restricted access).

Epping Forest is very much horse riding country. Where else more
fitting to erect a memorial to one's favourite steed?
  In the middle of a field in 'The Warren', stands this obelisk without

The Grosvenor Memorial to his horse.

any inscription. It serves as a memorial to the horse of General Thomas Grosvenor, (1764-1851),which died at the Battle of Waterloo in 1815. Grosvenor lived at the house on The Warren which is believed to have been visited by the Duke of Wellington, a close friend of the General.

In addition, there are many pleasant walks through this part of Epping.

Places of Interest in the Neighbourhood
Oldest Wooden Church (Greensted)
King Harold's Resting Place (Waltham Abbey)
A Fantasy Grotto (Wanstead)

Den of Tranquillity: John Child's Grotto.

80 A Fantasy Grotto

Position: Wanstead Park, Wanstead, Essex
OS Map: East London area, Sheet 177, 1:50,000
Map Ref: TQ 419 875
Access: Park on Wanstead Park Road (this runs parallel to the A406
South Woodford – Barking section). Cross the A406 by the footbridge
into the park. Passing over the stream, take the second footpath right to
the ornamental lake, keeping to the A406 side of the water. The grotto
lies across the lake at the point where it begins to widen.

Fantasy grottoes were all the rage among certain romantics in 18th
century England. The poet William Shenstone elaborates in his *Pastoral
Ballad;*

> My banks they are furnish'd with bees,
> Whose murmur invites one to sleep;
> My grottoes are shaded with trees,
> And my hills are white with sheep.

Wanstead may well have been a rural retreat when John Child, second
Earl Tylney, erected his grotto next to the ornamental lake. Originally,
it had arches, ancient Roman motifs, statues and an obelisk at its summit. Being purely for pleasure, it was adorned inside with sea shells of
many varieties. Pebbles and coloured glass enhanced the ceiling; all
glistened in the candlelight. It is reputed to have cost £40,000 – an
unbelievable extravagance in those days.

John Child died in 1784, and his grotto was badly damaged in a fire
exactly 100 years later. All that remains now are the overgrown ruins,
still romantically reflected in the lake.

Places of Interest in the Neighbourhood
Memorial to a Horse (Loughton)
King Harold's Resting Place (Waltham Abbey)

Index

Places by page number

Aldeburgh 75
Bacton 14
Blickling 35
Blythburgh 80
Bradwell-on-Sea 92, 117
Bungay 83
Burgh Castle 48
Burgh St Peter 40
Bury St Edmunds 52, 53, 54, 56,
  57, 58
Canewdon 92
Cawston 12
Colchester 99, 100, 102, 104, 105,
  107, 108
Dovercourt 91, 109
Dunwich 78
Earls Colne 94
East Bergholt 60
East Dereham 25
Edgefield 37
Elveden 50
Erwarton 63
Felsted 110, 111
Freston 64
Great Bardfield 92
Great Burstead 115
Great Wigborough 115
Great Yarmouth 27, 33
Greensted 118
Hempstead 86
Holbrook 62
Horringer 58
How Hill 28
Hoxne 81

Ipswich 84
King's Lynn 42, 44
Layer Marney 113
Little Dunmow 97
Little Ellingham 36
Little Wigborough 115
Long Melford 67
Loughton 123
Ludham 15, 28
Mistley 89
Moulton 51
Nacton 66
Norwich 11, 24, 29, 31
Parham 72
Pentlow 85
Rendlesham 70
Sible Hedingham 88
Stock 122
Stow Bartolph 47
Sudbury 59
Swaffham 39
Tattingstone 61
Thompson Common 17
Thorpeness 76
Waltham Abbey 121
Walton-on-the-Naze 95
Wanstead 125
Watton 17
Weeting 32
West Somerton 18
West Walton 45
Woodbridge 69
Wymondham 21, 23

The Curiosities of England

The following titles in the series have already been published and can be ordered at all bookshops, or in case of difficulties direct from the publishers.

Buckinghamshire Curiosities John Lucas 1 874336 11 3

Cheshire Curiosities Peter Bamford 0 946159 96 3

Cotswold Curiosities Reginald Dixon 0 946159 51 1

Dorset Curiosities George Osborn 0 946159 38 6

East Anglian Curiosities Rick O'Brien 0 946159 97 1

Hampshire Curiosities Jo Daper 0 946159 57 2

Hertfordshire Curiosities John Lucas 0 946159 75 0

Isle of Wight Curiosities Jack Jones 0 946159 67 X

Kent Curiosities John Vigar 0 946159 95 5

Lincolnshire Curiosities Howard Peach 1 874336 22 9

Northamptonshire Curiosities Chris Billing 1 874336 12 1

North and East Yorkshire Curiosities Duncan & Trevor Smith
  1 874336 09 1

Nottinghamshire Curiosities Geoffrey Oldfield 0 946159 98 X

Somerset Curiosities Enid Byford 0 946159 48 3

South and West Yorkshire Curiosities Duncan & Trevor Smith
  0 946159 99 8